FREEDOM FIGHTER

FREEDOM FIGHTER

*All Of Heaven Is In A Battle For All Of You–
A Battle For Your Whole Heart.*

CARRIE FULTON

XULON PRESS

Xulon Press
2301 Lucien Way #415
Maitland, FL 32751
407.339.4217
www.xulonpress.com

© 2020 by Carrie Fulton

All rights reserved solely by the author. The author guarantees all contents are original and do not infringe upon the legal rights of any other person or work. No part of this book may be reproduced in any form without the permission of the author. The views expressed in this book are not necessarily those of the publisher.

Unless otherwise indicated, Scripture quotations taken from the Holy Bible, New Living Translation (NLT). Copyright ©1996, 2004, 2007 by Tyndale House Foundation. Used by permission of Tyndale House Publishers, Inc.

Scripture quotations taken from the New King James Version (NKJV). Copyright © 1982 by Thomas Nelson, Inc. Used by permission. All rights reserved.

Scripture quotations taken from the New American Standard Bible (NASB). Copyright © 1960, 1962, 1963, 1968, 1971, 1972, 1973, 1975, 1977, 1995 by The Lockman Foundation. Used by permission. All rights reserved.

Scripture taken from The Passion Translation (TPT). Copyright © 2017 by Passion & Fire Ministries, Inc. Used by permission. All rights reserved. thePassionTranslation.com

Scripture quotations taken from the Holy Bible, New International Version (NIV). Copyright © 1973, 1978, 1984, 2011 by Biblica, Inc.™. Used by permission. All rights reserved.

Scripture quotations taken from The Holy Bible, Berean Study Bible (BSB). Copyright ©2016, 2018 by Bible Hub. Used by Permission. All Rights Reserved Worldwide.

Printed in the United States of America.

ISBN-13: 978-1-6305-0960-6

Dedication

I dedicate this book to my incredible tribe:
Grahm, thank you for empowering me to fearlessly pursue all the Father has intended for me. For teaching me to cast aside the opinions of others, while helping me find my roar. Your life has filled me with confidence.

Harper, thank you for awakening the sleeping giant of motherhood from within me. For unlocking inside me a capacity to love unselfishly, as never before. Your life has made me brave.

Ella Grace, thank you for teaching me about the beauty of wonder. We treasure the short time we were able to spend with you and can't wait for us all to be together again. Your life has inspired me to hope.

Abigail, thank you for teaching me about the redemptive grace-filled love of Christ. For showing me what beauty for ashes looks like. Your life helped liberate me from darkness.

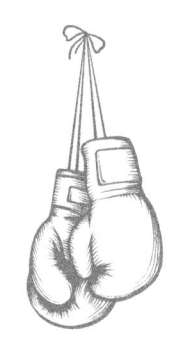

Table Of Contents

ACKNOWLEDGMENT ix

INTRODUCTION- xiii
The Summons to Transformation

BACK TO BEDROCK- 1
You are Destined for Promise

TESTING THE BLESSING- 7
Refining the Promise

FACING GIANTS 101- 15
Your Promise is a Weapon

WHOLEHEARTED- 23
Trusting in Your Promise

CAPTAIN OF THE HOSTS OF THE LORD- 29
Your Promise is a Roadmap

THE LION'S SHARE- 41
Unleashing the Roar of Heaven

DEFINING EZER- 51
Finding the Warrior Within

UNION RESERVOIR- 57
Introducing Destiny

DISCOVERY OF LOVE- 63
Awakening the Heart

CATCHING FOXES- 69
Slaying the Giants Within

BECAUSE HE SAYS SO- 91
The Transforming Power of His Love

DARK (K)NIGHT OF THE SOUL- 99
The Authority of Love

THE ENDGAME- 109
Being an Ambassador for Christ

SCOTOPLO- 119
Accosting the Darkness

CAGED NO MORE- 129
Restoring the Former Desolations

ADVANCING THE KINGDOM- 135
Gaining Momentum

PACKING A PUNCH, AN EPILOGUE- 145
A Journey in Prayer

ENDNOTES. 153

Acknowledgment

I have a two-year-old, and since my daughter was born, I have been a full-time stay at home mom, while also working part-time from home. One day, in the fall of 2019, the Lord told me to quit my part-time job because He had something else for me, though He did not share with me what it was. We were currently renting and had been trying to save money for a house. Quitting my job was not going to get us closer to our goal. However, obedience to the Lord is one of the most important things in my life. So, I obeyed and quit my job.

The time I previously spent working, while my daughter napped or late into the night when my family was asleep, I now used to spend time in the Word, as I awaited the Lord for more direction on what was next. I found myself devouring scripture, studying it deeper than I ever have before. It was during this time that I began to realize the Lord was asking me to write a book. Though He did not tell me what the book was to be about, I was confident He would show me what I needed to see, when I needed to see it.

Day after day, toddler nap after toddler nap, I would sit with the Holy Spirit and ask Him to show me what to write that day, and where to spend my focus. I leaned hard on the Holy Spirit. Even after getting a few chapters written, I wasn't totally sure what the message or point of the book would be. Nonetheless, I kept writing, trusting the Holy Spirit would help me.

Amid writing, I began to wonder how I would get this book published. I knew the Lord had a plan, but I did not know what the plan was. Coincidently, in January of 2020, I saw an advertisement for a Christian writing contest, hosted by a Christian publishing company. The contest required the entries be short stories of no more than 750 words. The first, second, and third place winners of the contest each received a publishing package. I went back and forth about whether to enter, but finally, a couple days before the deadline, I felt like I was supposed to. I took an excerpt from this book and reformatted it a bit to read more like a short story.

Up to this point, my husband was the only person who knew I was even working on a book. I didn't share with my husband, or anyone else, that I had entered the contest. Even though I felt led to enter it, I wasn't sure if anything would actually come of it and didn't want to own the rejection when I announced to my husband that I didn't win and wasted $39 on the entrance fee.

A few days after the deadline I found out I won third place. I cried and cried. Then I called my husband and shared about the contest with him, apologizing for not telling him about it. Winning for me not only validated that I had correctly discerned the Lord's voice to quit my other job, but it also encouraged me to keep going. To finish well.

Winning third place meant I won their basic publishing package. This package included formatting but not any actual distribution of the book. I was told I could apply the value of the package I won towards another package and pay the difference if I wanted. The next package up from mine would have cost me an additional $1,100.

During this time, we had just been informed our landlord was raising our rent when our lease expired in two months. Unable to renew our lease at the new rate, we had been frantically trying to find a new place to rent. We could not find an apartment complex within 50 miles who would rent to us because our dog is a Pitbull.

Acknowledgment

    I had been unemployed for the last three months working on this book which meant we had not been saving any money. We were in a very challenging situation to say the least. Consequently, I did not feel right taking any of the money we had been saving for a house to 'buy up' a better package, even though my husband said he was open to discussing it. It had already cost my family so much for me to obey the Lord in writing this book. With everything else we were facing, it simply felt like too much to ask anything else of them.

    While I knew I was obeying the Lord to write this book, quitting my job, and consequently not earning any more money, was hard for me. I would watch my husband leave for work every morning and feel guilty I wasn't doing more, despite knowing I was obeying the Lord. So, I didn't push the matter any further about buying-up a package.

    I reasoned, 'the Lord has brought this book this far, if He wants to take it further, I can trust Him for it.'

    I spoke with my publisher on Thursday and told her where we stood. She informed me that if I thought I would change my mind, I should let her know by tomorrow (Friday), because they were planning to raise their prices on Monday.

    "Thanks," I thought to myself, "I really needed one more obstacle right now."

    The next day (Friday) my mom and dad stopped by our house. They did not know any of this was going on, and I hadn't told them I was writing a book yet. My parents told me that my mom had received an unexpected bonus at work, and they felt impressed to share it with us. They handed us a check for a $1,000. The very amount I needed to buy-up the next package so my book could be distributed!

    I felt this was a timely gift from the Lord to 'buy up' the next package but I wanted to make sure my husband felt the same way. I told him my parents had given us $1,000 but didn't say anything further about the book. My parents had also decided to treat us to a weekend away in the mountains for some skiing and family fun together.

My parents and I drove up Friday morning and the plan was for Grahm to meet up with us after work. There was a white-out blizzard that day and they closed the mountain pass right after we made it through. Grahm would not be able to join us until the next morning.

Eight o'clock Friday evening, Grahm texted me and said, "I think we should use the money your parents gave us to 'buy up' the package for your book."

I thought my heart was going to explode. I was overjoyed we were on the same page, while also frantically trying to contact the publisher to see if we had made the deadline before the price increase. I did not hear back from the publisher until Monday morning, but they agreed to honor the previous price for us. The package we purchased is currently valued at $4,500- of which we paid $100.

I went from writing a book and having no idea how I would get it published or distributed, to a book that will be available for international distribution. The book you are holding is a miracle work from God; He filled the pages and He paid the way for it. He filled the pages, and He paid the way for it. My name is on the cover, but it should be the Lord's. As I've looked back on what's written in the pages of this book, I've realized my entire life has been in preparation for this one moment.

I have no idea what will come of it, if anything- but I hope more than just my mom purchases it. I hope it helps to replace some of the income my family has lost so that I could 'birth' it. I hope it teaches people about God's intentionality and overwhelming faithfulness. I hope it ignites a revival and helps fuel reformation. But more than anything, I hope it shows people how fiercely loved they really are.

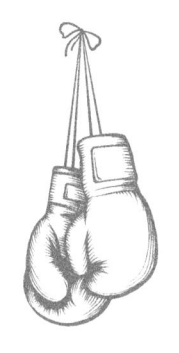

INTRODUCTION -
The Summons To Transformation

I was recently playing Super Mario Brothers on Wii with my mom and nephews. We were fighting desperately to rescue Princess Peach, but the mushrooms and turtles were getting the better of us. After much effort, we had each failed at our attempt to rescue the princess.

I yelled out, "It's okay, sometimes you have to die to live!"

We all laughed at this. It made no sense. Death is the antithesis to life. The game was over. There is, however, another kind of 'death' we should not overlook. More than death, it is an opportunity for true life. A life that is totally transformed by Jesus Christ.

The best example of transformation we see in nature is the butterfly. It starts out as an egg, growing on the very leaf it will soon digest. Once it hatches, it is a tiny caterpillar whose main goal is to consume as much food as possible, for growth. When the caterpillar has reached the perfect size, it spins a chrysalis, cocooning itself.

Externally there is no tangible sign of life. From within though, the caterpillar is working tirelessly to digest itself. Each body part the caterpillar has must be transformed. All of it needs to endure metamorphosis.

When the transformation is complete, the butterfly will emerge from the chrysalis. It will remain there as long as it needs, in order to pump blood thoroughly into its wings. It has no power or ability to fly without this blood transfusion. When this is complete, it takes flight, becoming what it was always meant to be. Free.

What inspires me most about our friend the butterfly are not its beautiful wings nor its newfound freedom. It is that it chooses to undergo this transformation. It chooses to breakdown its current identity, digesting itself from the inside out, to become what it was always meant to be. The formerly earthbound caterpillar is now a beautiful fluttering symbol of transformation, and dare I say resurrection.

We are meant to do the same. If we really want to step into all God has destined for us, then we all must make the brave journey of shedding our current 'identity.' We must bravely transition from always needing to be rescued, like Princess Peach, into our destiny as the triumphant Bride of Christ. This book is meant to be a guide, to help you on your journey of transformation to the Bride of Christ.

I am not pretending this process is without pain, however, I have come to realize it costs us far more not to transform. We were never meant to sluggishly creep through life. We were meant to be transformed and transfused by His blood- His redeeming love.

I have been devouring Song of Songs lately- studying the transformation and growth of the Shulamite, a biblical symbol for the Bride of Christ. The book begins with the bride fully aware of her own darkness and sin. She addresses it constantly in fact. It is beautiful to me though, that while all she can see is her darkness, all He ever addresses is her light. Her destiny.

In the middle of the book, she finally realizes that not only is she meant to have all of Him, but He also desires all of her. Even her darkness. At this realization she cries out, "Then may your awakening breath blow upon my life until I am fully yours. Breathe upon me with your Spirit wind. Stir up the sweet spice of your life within me. Spare nothing as you make me your fruitful garden. Hold nothing back until I release your fragrance…Come walk with me until I am fully yours" (Song of Songs 4:16-5:1; TPT).

The Summons To Transformation

It is on the heels of this prayer anthem that He proclaims she is finally ready to fly. His life within her is now a feast offering to the nations, as He declares all the fruits of His life are now found inside her. She is finally free, as she embraces what she was always meant to be. His.

As she steps into the fullness of this eternal identity, this destiny of love, she is now equipped to run with Him. To storm the forgotten places and gather the exiles back to Him. To restore the Lord's children back to Himself. To reestablish God's family and God's governmental rule in the earth.

With these things in mind, we will spend the first portion of this book detailing the importance of identity and the power of walking in covenant relationship with God. We will also learn how to use our covenants and promises as a weapon in spiritual warfare, while I reveal strategic battleplans for us, tucked within the Old Testament.

From this foundation, we will build our understanding of covenant relationship with Him as we walk through Song of Songs. Song of Songs is not a book just for women. While it uses bridal language, it is a metaphor for the entire Body of Christ. It is a roadmap for us, highlighting the process of transformation we all must bravely choose, as we grow in becoming the Bride of Christ. It will teach us how to let His love slay the giants hiding in our hearts, while also commissioning us to the mandate of our co-inheritance.

Mike Bickle says, "When Jesus returns, He is returning to a Church. Yes, they are sons of God. Yes, they are in the family of God. Yes, they are the Body of Christ AND they are in their bridal identity as a Bride saying, 'Come, Lord Jesus. We know who we are to You now. Come, we know who You are [to us]. The essence of the message of the Bride of Christ is the revelation of Jesus' beauty, His emotions for us, His commitments to share His heart, throne, secrets, and beauty with us as our Bridegroom King, and our response of wholehearted love and obedience to Him."[1]

We will spend the last section of the book discussing the mandate we now have as the Beloved. A mandate to be a light in darkness, to reestablish God's family, to restore the exiles, and to rebuild His kingdom- on earth as it is in Heaven. I will share powerful testimonies from my own life and journey with the Lord to help illustrate some of this, and to also serve as a launchpad for anyone else needing breakthrough or personal revival.

I serve a miracle working God. I believe, with all that I am, that nothing is impossible for Him. God is not limited to our understanding of Him, of biology, or of time and space. Our limited beliefs, however, can keep us bound like a sluggish caterpillar. Bound from experiencing His fullness and our destiny.

"There is nothing impossible with God. All the impossibility is with us when we measure God by the limitations of our unbelief" (Smith Wigglesworth).

Jesus paid an ultimate price to obtain an ultimate victory. I don't ever want to impose my human limitations on a God this big. Like Peter, I would much prefer to boldly step out of the boat, running the risk of looking foolish or sinking, than to sit back in fear and apathy, always wondering what could have been. I would rather boldly believe the Lord without limits and embrace the potential for being misunderstood and rejected, than to cower life away on the cave of my sofa, never knowing my full potential in Christ.

I believe we are at a tipping point in the Body of Christ. I believe the glory is pressing down from Heaven, waiting for a people who will extend their hands and partner with Heaven. Waiting for a bride who will boldly see all that Jesus died for to become manifest on the earth. It is time to enlarge the tent of our understanding, and our very expectancy. We are the Bride of Christ.

"For whoever wants to save his life will lose it, but whoever loses his life for My sake will save it" (Luke 9:24).

Revelation 11:15 announces to us that the kingdom of the world (nations) will become the Kingdom of our Lord, and He will reign forever. We often hear people say, 'with great authority comes great responsibility.' Our responsibility to Revelation 11:15 is to become a people who can be trusted with His authority. The plumb line for this is birthed on the wings of love and surrender.

We become this when we are able to fully identify with Galatians 2:20, "I have been crucified with Christ; and it is no longer I who live, but Christ lives in me; and the life which I now live in the flesh I live by faith in the Son of God, who loved me and gave Himself up for me."

I hope this book helps you on your journey of letting Him lead you in who you were always meant to be. Of equal importance, I hope it empowers you on your journey of letting Him love you. Heidi Baker says, "You have no authority where you have no love."

Living loved is the greatest thing we could hope to accomplish in this life. It wrecks violence on the enemy and empowers an otherwise sleeping giant- His bride. Jesus paid for that to be a reality for us. To not fully accept all that His crucifixion paid the price for would be a grave disappointment. Pun intended.

Let's take a lesson from our friend the butterfly and become what we were always meant to be. Let's let His blood pump through our wings so to speak, until at last we are able to soar in Him.

BACK TO BEDROCK
You Are Destined For Promise

If you are born again, you are in covenant with the Lord. Covenants are one of the many special gifts the Lord gives to us. Within them, the Lord offers us all that He is, and all His resources-often only requiring of us that we simply choose to believe He will be faithful to accomplish it.

If you study the covenants in the Bible, you will see that every single one is meant for our good. Within every single one, the Lord is giving us a promise, while simultaneously releasing provision and inheritance of some sort. When we keep our covenants with the Lord, we are strengthened, empowered, victorious, and protected. When we stand firm on them, it unleashes our inheritance. When we abandon them, we invite chaos, war, and ruin into our lives.

Even when we do not obey, and break covenant with Him, He provides a way for us still. We see this in 1 Kings 8:33-34, "When Your people Israel are defeated before an enemy, because they have sinned against You, if they turn to You again and confess Your name and pray and make supplication to You in this hour, then hear in heaven, and forgive the sin of Your people Israel, and bring them back to the land which You gave to their fathers."

His abundance is overwhelmingly in our favor. It is simply up to us to obey.

John Piper says this about covenant, "In almost every case He comes to the covenant partner, lays His job description out and says, 'This is how I will work for you with all My heart and with all My soul and with all My strength, if you will love Me as I am, cleave to Me, and trust Me to keep My word.'"[2]

One example of covenant in the Old Testament was the Ark of the Covenant. The book of Exodus introduces us to the Ark of the Covenant, or Ark of the Testimony, depending on your Bible translation. The Ark of the Covenant testified to the agreement God made with the Israelites at Mount Sinai. It also represented the presence of God with His people and His accompanying power. It allowed the opportunity for God and man to meet, and for the sins of man to be atoned for before the Lord, once a year, on the Day of Atonement.

The ark itself was a box which housed the stone tablets Moses used to write the Ten Commandments (testimony of covenant). The lid to the ark was called the mercy seat, which was then canopied by the wings of two cherubim facing each other with their wings stretched out.

The ark was kept behind a veil in the tabernacle, and later the temple, in a room known as the Holy of Holies. It could only be visited once a year, on the Day of Atonement, and only by the high priest. The high priest had to follow specific rules in order to enter, including animal sacrifice for the atonement of mans' sins. If any of the rules were not followed, the high priest would be struck dead. There were a lot less people applying to be head pastors back then.

"The cherubim shall have their wings spread upwards, covering the mercy seat with their wings facing one another; the faces of the cherubim are to be turned toward the mercy seat. You shall put the mercy seat on top of the ark, and in the ark you shall put the testimony which I will give to you. There I will meet with you; and from above the mercy seat, from between the two cherubim which are upon the Ark of the Testimony, I will speak to you about all that I will give you in commandment for the sons of Israel" (Exodus 25: 20-22).

The Hebrew word used for "ark" in Deuteronomy 10 is the same as that used in Genesis 50:26, when we read of the "coffin" of Joseph. Why would the Lord do this? Why would He place the Ten Commandments (testimony of covenant) inside a coffin (ark), top it with a mercy seat, cover it with cherubim, and then promise His presence to be manifested between the mercy seat and the cherubim?

He is pointing us towards a foreshadowing of Jesus Christ, our Messiah, the atoner of our sins. The Lord always intended for the law of animal sacrifice to be temporary, to prepare the way for Jesus. Jesus dealt a decisive death blow to Satan's hold over man, which had come about because of our sin. Jesus put to death the law requiring lifeblood as repayment for our sins by offering himself as a sinless sacrifice in our place. A once and for all payment for sin. Now all we must do is believe.

"But when Christ appeared as a high priest of the good things to come, He entered through the greater and more perfect tabernacle, not made with hands, that is to say, not of this creation; and not through the blood of goats and calves, but through His own blood, He entered the holy place once and for all, having obtained eternal redemption" (Hebrews 9:11-12).

Jesus established for our atonement, a new covenant by which everyone can find atonement for the payment of their sins through faith in Jesus Christ, God's risen Son. "For God so loved the world, that He gave His only begotten Son, that whoever believes in Him shall not perish, but have eternal life" (John 3:16).

I find it fascinating the priests were to only wear linen garments when ministering to the Lord in the holy of holies so they would not sweat. Sweating is a sign of human effort, a sign of work. Thanks to Jesus, we do not work to earn grace. His grace is freely given.

"For by grace you have been saved through faith and that not of yourselves, it is the gift of God, not as a result of works, so that no one may boast. For we are His workmanship, created in Christ Jesus for good works, which God prepared beforehand that we should walk in them" (Ephesians 2:8-10).

Jesus has become our mercy seat. A once and for all payment for all our sins, so that we may have fellowship and access to the presence of God. Jesus is the only way to eternal life. Full stop. I have heard a lot of people propose there is more than one way to get to Heaven or think we all end up there in the end, regardless of what you believe. I find Bill Johnson's response to this brilliant, "If that is true, then what God required of Jesus (the crucifixion) was unusually cruel."

Jesus is the only way.

The Old Testament model of the Ark of Covenant- with the Ten Commandments (testimony of covenant) in a coffin (ark), covered by a mercy seat, overshadowed with cherubim, and the promise of His hovering presence above the mercy seat, is our Old Covenant with the Lord.

Our New Covenant is the crucifixion of Jesus Christ. The New Testament model of the Ark of Covenant is Jesus himself. The death of Christ on the cross, symbolizing the coffin, taking back the keys from Satan as the spotless lamb, thereby paying our debt for sin- our testimony within the coffin.

Death could not hold him as He rose from the grave to show us mercy (mercy seat), overshadowed by the angels who rolled away the stone (cherubim), and then sending the promised Holy Spirit, effectively upgrading our relationship with Him. We went from a people whom the presence of God hovered over, to a people indwelt by the presence of the Holy Spirit.

The Bible makes it clear that Christ was chosen before the creation of the world for the accomplishment of this very task. "God chose Him as your ransom long before the world began, but now in these last days He has been revealed for your sake" (1 Peter:1:20; NLT).

This was not God's plan B. This was always meant to be, before the Lord ever started creating creation. Jesus Christ, the perfect and spotless Lamb, would be crucified for us. Why? Love is the innermost answer. God is not governed by time as we are. He knows the beginning from the end. He is the Alpha and the Omega- living fully at both ends of eternity. Because of this, He knew there could be only one way.

He loves you that fiercely. He loves His children with an intensity even the grave cannot hold. He knows the frailty of our humanity and knew we would need His help. He is a good Father.

"Keep the charge of the Lord your God, to walk in His ways, to keep His statutes, His commandments, His ordinances, and His testimonies, according to what is written in the Law of Moses, that you may succeed in all that you do and wherever you turn" (1 Kings 2:3).

We learn even more about God's fierce love when we study Revelation 12. It starts out with a woman (Israel) in great pain, giving birth. As she is in labor, the red dragon (Satan) is standing before her, waiting for the child to be birthed so he can devour it. She gives birth to a son (Christ), and the child is caught up to God and to His throne before the dragon can devour it.

Next, Michael and his angels wage war with Satan and Satan's army. Satan's army is not strong enough and he and his army are thrown out of Heaven and cast down to earth. From here, we pick up the story in Revelation 12:10: "Then I heard a loud voice in heaven saying, "Now the salvation, and the power, and the kingdom of our God and the authority of His Christ have come, for the accuser of our brethren has been thrown down, he who accuses them before our God day and night. And they overcame him because of the blood of the Lamb and because of the word of their testimony, and they did not love their life even when faced with death."

This passage tells us that we overcome the enemy by the blood of the Lamb and by the word of our testimony. How? Because the "testimony of Jesus is the spirit of prophecy" (Revelation 19:10). When we give testimony of Jesus, we release a faith into the atmosphere to see His victory enforced again in a situation. In Hebrew, the word 'testimony,' comes from a word that means, 'to remember, repeat, or do again.' When you give testimony to what Jesus has done, you release a power into the atmosphere for that testimony to be repeated. This is why it is imperative we open our mouths and share what the Lord has done for us. We need to share our testimonies and share the gospel and watch as His power manifest in the world around us.

"…And this truth of who I am will be the bedrock foundation on which I will build my church – my legislative assembly, and the power of death will not be able to overpower it! I will give you the keys of heaven's kingdom realm to forbid on earth that which is forbidden in heaven, and to release on earth that which is released in heaven" (Matthew 16:18; TPT).

We know from Ephesians 6:12 that we do not war against flesh and blood but against rulers of darkness. With the cross in mind, we are meant to enforce His victory on earth, as it is in heaven. If not, why else are we here? With the cross, God could have just raptured us all and called it a day. He didn't. He has commissioned us to push back the darkness and bring His kingdom into the earth. Why? So the fullness of His love can be made known.

"Lord, I passionately love you and I'm bonded to you, for now you've become my power! You're as real to me as bedrock beneath my feet, like a castle on a cliff, my forever firm fortress, my mountain of hiding, my pathway of escape, my tower of rescue where none can reach me. My secret strength and shield around me, you are salvation's ray of brightness shining on the hillside, always the champion of my cause. All I need to do is to call to you, singing to you, the praiseworthy God. When I do, I'm safe and sound in you" (Psalm 18:1-3; TPT).

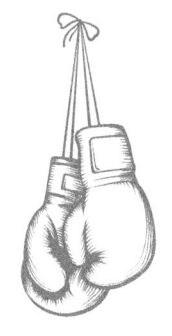

TESTING THE BLESSING
Refining The Promise

When God speaks, it will always come to pass. Whenever God gives a blessing, a promise, or a purpose- it will manifest. The Bible tells us we were established before the foundation of the world, in the mind and heart of God. Before we were even born, He created each one of us with a distinct purpose.

"Before I formed you in the womb I knew you, and before you were born I set you apart and appointed you as a prophet to the nations...for I am watching over my word to accomplish it" (Jeremiah 1:5,12).

What can we expect then? Proverbs 30:5 tells us, "Every word of God is tested; He is a shield to those who take refuge in Him."

Every promise He gives must be refined in the fire, until all doubt and wavering are purged away, and the Word is proven true. When those refining fires of testing come, we must lean on our promise, the faithfulness of God, and let the Lord be our shield through the testing. We need to surround ourselves with hope, putting our trust in His ability to birth the impossible.

I have come to understand that nearly every problem or obstacle in my life has ultimately led me to realize what the Lord is asking me through the situation: "Do you trust Me?"

In these spaces of my history, I would do well to remember that grapes must be pressed to make wine, diamonds form under pressure, pearls form as the result of an invading irritant, olives must be crushed to produce oil, the caterpillar must digest itself to become the butterfly, and seeds grow in darkness.

As God brings His promises into our lives, they will nearly always have to endure the crucifix of testing, and your faith regarding what God has given you, will be tested along with it. God has a way of giving you a dream or a promise and then asking you to believe for the supernatural, so that it might come to pass, as you endure the fight of faith in embracing your promise. How else are you supposed to learn that He is faithful?

We are all in some form of process as we hold onto something God has purposed for us, whether we realize it or not. Even Jesus had to endure this. The Holy Spirit led Him into the wilderness to be tested by Satan, when Jesus had been fasting for 40 days.

"Then Jesus was led up by the Spirit into the wilderness to be tempted by the devil. And after He had fasted forty days and forty nights, He then became hungry. And the tempter came and said to Him, "If You are the Son of God, command that these stones become bread." But He answered and said, "it is written, 'Man shall not live on bread alone, but on every word that proceeds out of the mouth of God'" (Matthew 4:1-4).

Interestingly, the number forty usually signifies passing a test or enduring a trial. After Jesus was tempted for forty days, he passed the test, and returned from the wilderness filled with power. He then entered the synagogue and read Isaiah 61, declaring, "Today this Scripture is fulfilled in your hearing." And he sat down.

Jewish tradition holds that synagogues had a special seat reserved only for the returning Messiah. When Jesus finished reading the scroll of Isaiah 61, this was the seat He went and sat in. Proclaiming to everyone in earshot that He was in fact their promised Messiah. The One they had been waiting for. They didn't receive Him though. In fact, they all became outraged with Him and sought to throw Him over the cliff, but the Bible says He passed through the crowd unharmed and left.

If you keep reading about the temptation of Jesus, the passage from Matthew 4, you will find Satan continued to tempt Jesus two more times. He tempted Him to leap from a pinnacle and rely on angels to break His fall, and to kneel before Satan in return for all the kingdoms of the world. It is interesting to me that Satan tempts Jesus with things that are already His, or soon will be. Satan was offering Jesus a shortcut to His promise. However, Jesus knew the crucifix of testing was the only way to truly behold His promise. The same is true for us.

We must go through something so we can know for ourselves how wonderful, powerful, faithful, and magnificent He really is. We must learn to trust Him for ourselves. We need to know that we have access to Him. We need to know He is abundantly relational, and we are important to Him. He is willing to accost our comfort zones and take us through things we do not like, so we can learn more about Him.

"Dear friends, don't be surprised at the fiery trials you are going through, as if something strange were happening to you. Instead, be very glad for these trials make you partners with Christ in his suffering, so that you will have the wonderful joy of seeing His glory when it is revealed to all the world" (1 Peter 4:12-13; NLT).

The word 'rejoice' in this verse is the Greek word '*chairete*.' It is a primary verb and one of the definitions for it is 'to be well.' When you find yourself in the midst of testing, are you able to put your trust in His word and declare 'it is well with my soul?'

I want to highlight for you a woman in the Bible who was able to do just that. The Bible calls her a 'great woman,' though we are never given the pleasure of knowing her name. It is the story of the Shunammite woman, found in 2 Kings 4.

We will pick up the story with Elisha passing back forth through Shunem, a town that means 'double resting place,' on his way to

Mount Carmel. The Shunamite woman observes him traveling back and forth through the town and persuades him to stop at her house and eat as he passes by. She would not take "no" for an answer. And so, every time he passes through Shunem, he stops at her house to eat.

We don't know how much time passes but eventually she approaches her husband, and shares with him that she perceives Elisha is a holy man of God. She asks her husband if they can make a room for him on top of their house, so he can have a place to turn in. Her husband agrees and they build a studio apartment for Elisha on top of their house.

After some time, Elisha has grown quite comfortable with resting in this room they have prepared just for him. He calls his servant, Gehazi, and asks him to bring the Shunammite to him. As she is standing in front of both of them, Elisha says, "...Behold, you have been careful for us with all this care; what can I do for you?"

She responds by telling him she is content. She has not done all these things for them in hopes of yielding any sort of return. She simply wanted to bless them. After she leaves, Elisha asks Gehazi for ideas on how they might bless her. 'Gehazi' means 'valley of vision.' Gehazi mentions his former observation that she has no son and her husband is advanced in age. He can see, in the midst of her valley, a vision for her life.

In those days, if you were childless, you didn't have anything. It was shameful not to have children. They were your blessing and your inheritance. In that culture, the ideal family was one with sons, because they carried on the family line. Women wanted to be mothers more than anything else, they wanted to continue their family line.

The Shunammite was childless. We can assume they likely tried for years to conceive, possibly embracing countless miscarriages, or nagging infertility. After years of disappointment, she probably abandoned all hope she would ever have a child.

With the revelation Gehazi shared, Elisha calls her back. As she's standing in the doorway, he tells her that this time next year, she will embrace a son. She responds in verse 16, "No, my lord, O man of God, do not lie to your maidservant."

In other words, 'could it really be true? Dare I hold hope again and believe for a child of my own? Please don't breathe hope on my heart without truly bringing it to pass! I don't think I could bear anymore disappointment here.'

It happened exactly as Elisha promised and a year later, she was holding her son. Several years pass, and the child suddenly becomes ill. He says to his father in verse 19, "My head! My head!" His father doesn't know what to do so he tells the servants to take the boy to his mother. The Bible tells us the boy sits on his mother's lap ill, and then at noon, the boy dies.

'Noon' in this passage comes from the word *'tsohar.'* It means 'light or double light.' It is derived from the words *'tsahar'* and *'yitshar'* which mean 'to press out oil, anointed.' Olive trees are the only trees that convert water to oil, and they are considered small evergreen trees. Evergreen trees are a symbol of eternal covenant. Abraham planted an evergreen tree as a sign of the covenant God had made with him in Genesis 21:33.

Olives must be pressed to produce olive oil. The death of the Shunammite's son pressed down on her, drawing out oil, drawing out grace to believe for the impossible. Drawing out faith to believe in the promise of God.

Olive oil is mentioned a lot throughout scripture and the olive branch is a symbol of peace. To extend an olive branch was to extend peace, to end hostility between two parties, signaling the end of a conflict. The United Nations flag contains an olive branch for this very reason; to end all hostilities between waring nations. It's also on the 1885 Great Seal of the United States. The Father extended the Prince of Peace for our sake, to end the hostility of sin and make a way of peace for us.

So, she decides to stand on the promise of peace and the power of covenant and takes her son to Elisha's room. She lays him on

Elisha's bed and closes the door. She asks her husband to send her one of the servants and one of the donkeys, that she may run after Elisha. Her husband doesn't understand why. He questions her in verse 23 about why he should do this. It wasn't a day for church and besides, didn't they have a son to bury?

She responds in verse 23, "It will be well."

When the Shunammite tells her husband, 'it will be well,' this phrase comes from the original word *'shalom.'* It means 'completeness, peace, to be well, perfect, in good health.' This is the same word used to describe Jesus as the Prince of Peace in Isaiah 9:6, "For unto us a Child is born, unto us a son is given; and the government will be upon His shoulder. And His name will be called Wonderful, Counselor, Mighty God, Everlasting Father, Prince of Peace."

She mounts the donkey and commands the servant to push the donkey forward, hard, and not to slow down unless she tells him to. She finds Elisha at Mount Carmel. He sees her at a distance and asks Gehazi to run out and meet her and ask if it is well with her, her husband and her child. Gehazi obeys.

She responds, "it is well."

When the Shunammite finds Elisha at Mount Carmel, she bows at his feet and says, "…Did I not say, 'Do not deceive me?'"

She had hope he could help her, amid feeling somewhat betrayed. 'Mount Carmel' means 'garden, vineyard, orchard.' This highlights for us Jesus in the Garden of Gethsemane. 'Gethsemane' means 'oil press,' and we know the Garden of Gethsemane was an olive grove. Gethsemane was also the place where Jesus was betrayed by Judas. The weight of our sin that Jesus experienced in Gethsemane pressed down on Him, and the Bible tells us He was up all night interceding for us. Praying so hard, He sweat blood.

At the response of the Shunammite woman, Elisha instructs Gehazi to gird his loins, go out ahead of them, and take his staff and lay it on the boy's face. Gehazi does as Elisha instructs but nothing happens. Gehazi reports back that the boy has not awakened.

Interestingly, 'awakened' in this verse is derived from a word that means 'harvest.'

Elisha finally arrives at the house, enters his room, closes the door, and prays to the Lord. Elisha lays on the boy, putting his mouth on the boy's mouth, his eyes on the boy's eyes, and his hands on the boy's hands. He stretches himself out on the boy. He feels the boy's body become warm, and then the boy sneezes seven times, and opens his eyes. He calls the Shunammite in and tells her to take her son.

Most scholars seem to agree she had two possible routes for getting to Elisha in Mount Carmel, one being 32 miles and the other being twenty miles. Donkeys can usually only travel 4-5 miles a day. They are slow animals and can only gallop in short bursts, though not likely with a rider onboard. This means it would have taken the Shunammite four to six days to reach Elisha at Carmel. And another four to six days for them to return to her home.

Science tells us that after a body has been dead for eight to ten days, the internal organs have decomposed, the body starts to bloat, and bloody foam leak from the mouth and nose. The body turns from green to red as the blood decomposes and the organs in the abdomen accumulate gas and the body begins to digest itself.[3]

Elisha finds the boy in this state and lays on the boy, mouth to mouth, eye to eye, hand to hand. Just think about that for a moment. It's no wonder the boy sneezed seven times, he had a lot of liquid to clear out of his airway.

Can you even begin to imagine this whole story? She's holding her promise in her arms, and it dies. The blessing she didn't ask for is dead. A blessing she never thought she'd have but always longed for is dead. Beautifully though, something on the inside of her says, "it's not over. I am not burying my promise. I didn't ask for this. God gave me this. If God gave me this, I don't believe God will just let it die. This is my covenant, my promise from the Lord. This can't be the end."

Loren Larson says, "When something supernatural is given, it will be supported by the supernatural faith that is not accompanied when we lose things we worked for. When it's something God did, even when it looks like it's dead, you can expect God to do something unexpected. You can expect the impossible. The gift of faith looks death in the eye and declares life."

Something within her would not let go of this promise, despite all odds. If something has come against your promise, it is not a time for the promise to be over. It is a time of testing. You will have to go through something, to come out with something. When you are born again, you become one with Christ. You are immersed in Him. This means we aren't trying to get to Elisha, like the Shunammite, but rather the cross, like Jesus.

It's interesting to me all of this occurs in a place described as a 'double resting place,' at a time of day called 'double light,' by a prophet with a double portion anointing on his life, whose name means 'God is my salvation.'

Isaiah 61:7 tells us, "Instead of your shame you will have a double portion, and instead of humiliation they will shout for joy over their portion. Therefore they will possess a double portion in their land, Everlasting joy will be theirs."

Take your trials to the cross. Immerse them in who He is until you can say, 'it is well.' In that place, you will find that you are in your answer. You are submerged in Him. Submerge your trial in Him as well. Life on the water with Jesus is always far safer than being in the boat without Him.

"Great faith is the product of great fights. Great testimonies are the outcome of great tests. Great triumphs can only come out of great trials" (Smith Wigglesworth).

Battles are not about circumstances. Battles are about trust, and trust is built on covenant.

FACING GIANTS 101
Your Promise Is A Weapon

When I mention 'David and Goliath,' do memories of Sunday school felt boards flood your mind? Do you imagine a small boy, a sling, and a giant? Truly, this is another story we need to revisit in the Bible, one which beautifully illustrates the power of standing on your covenant promises as a weapon against the enemy.

I recently heard a sermon by Dutch Sheets that helped me realize there was so much about David and Goliath I did not know. He shared in the sermon that David had conducted the battle against Goliath based on his history and his covenant promises with the Lord.

To refresh, the story begins with the Philistine army gathered for battle on one side of the mountain, while the Israelite army stood on the other side of the mountain, with the valley of Elah between them. These two armies have been gathered here for forty days, and all they've managed to do is shout at each other. Goliath steps forward and challenges Israel to send forth their champion for a battle against Goliath. Goliath proposes that if he wins, the Israelites will serve the Philistines. But if the Israelites win, the Philistines will serve Israel.

When Saul and all Israel heard this, they were overcome with fear. Day after day, for forty days straight, they would gather, shout at each other, and then Goliath would come forward and take his stand- taunting someone to challenge him. All of Israel was far too afraid. And for forty days straight, Israel retreated at the intimidation of Goliath.

David was the youngest son of Jesse. Jesse's three oldest sons had followed Saul to the battle and had been gone for forty days. Jesse sent David to the battle to deliver supplies and to report back on the condition of his brothers. When David approached his brothers, they reproached him, assuming he was there to mock them.

Some suggest that Goliath wasn't the real giant David had to defeat that day, but rather the mockery of his older brothers…'why don't you go back and look after your few little sheep' (verse 28). David's brothers despised him. He was the smallest one in their tribe and viewed by them as the most insignificant. He would have to push past their reproach if he was going to step into his destiny.

He does, and David arrives to the battle just in time to hear Goliath come forward and taunt Israel for a challenger. The Israelites flee the battle line in fear of Goliath, for the fortieth time. At this David asks in verse 26, "What will be done for the man who kills the Philistine and takes away the reproach from Israel? For who is this uncircumcised Philistine, that he should taunt the armies of the living God?"

David approaches Saul and tells him not to fear, he will go and fight the Philistine himself. Think about this for a second- a boy is telling a king not to be afraid. Saul rebukes David and tells him he can't fight the Philistine because he is only a boy, while Goliath has been a warrior since he was a boy.

David responds back to Saul, telling him of how he looks after his sheep. Sharing he has killed the lion and the bear to protect his sheep and the uncircumcised Philistine will meet the same fate, since he has taunted the armies of the living God.

"The Lord who delivered me from the paw of the lion and from the paw of the bear, He will deliver me from the hand of this Philistine" (1 Samuel 17: 37).

Upon hearing this, Saul grants David permission. Saul tries to clothe David in his battle armor, but it is far too big. David gives them back and tells Saul he can't use them because he has not 'tested them.' This is a great reminder for us to be who God made us to be and not someone else. You will have victory only as you be who God has made you to be.

David grabs his staff and chooses five smooth stones from the brook and puts them in his pouch. With his staff in one hand and his sling in the other, he approached the Philistine giant. Goliath is outraged when he sees that his challenger is but a youth. He taunts David.

David responds with, "You come to me with a sword, a spear, and a javelin, but I come to you in the name of the Lord of hosts, the God of the armies of Israel, whom you have taunted. This day the Lord will deliver you up into my hands, and I will strike you down and remove your head from you...that all this assembly may know that the Lord does not deliver by sword or by spear; for the battle is the Lord's and He will give you into our hands" (1 Samuel 17:45-47).

Next, they charge towards each other and David hurls the stone, striking Goliath on the forehead and killing him. David then draws Goliath's sword from its sheath and cuts his head off with it.

Reflecting back, Dutch Sheets explains, "David conducted that whole battle based on his history...When David says, "is there not a cause?" Cause can mean 'history.' In other words, David may have literally been saying to his brother, 'is there not a history? Aren't there some promises in our past that give us the power and authority of heaven to deal with this giant?" ...Judah was David's tribe. So, what David is really saying is, 'you know why I am going to win this battle? Because this is my land. Given to me by God and you can't have my land. I have a divine right to this land, and you are trespassing.'"[4]

Shepherds always carried two sticks with them when they were looking after sheep. A shorter stick, called a 'rod,' was used to fight off wild dogs and other predators. The other stick they carried was called a 'staff.' The staff was usually longer than the rod and had a curved hook at one end. The staff was used to lead the sheep, as well as to rescue them when they wandered where they shouldn't or got stuck. They could wrap the hook around the sheep's neck and pull it off a dangerous cliff, out of a sinkhole or mud pit, or help redirect the sheep whenever needed.

We know David was a shepherd. Rick Clendenen shares this about shepherds: "In Bible times shepherds had a unique way of displaying their testimony. As part of the passage of manhood, each young shepherd was given his own staff. He used that staff not only to shepherd sheep, but also to chronicle the victories of his life. It became a symbol of his testimony carried in his hand." [5]

We can assume a shepherd's life is a nomadic one, with many nights spent around a fire with other shepherds. Surely to pass the time, shepherds would have spent a great deal of their time together sharing the stories behind the carvings on their staffs. Shepherds would have shared their victories with each other, repeatedly, solidifying within themselves their very ability to shepherd.

We have the advantage of knowing some of what would have been carved on David's staff: covenant relationship with God, tribe of Judah, shepherding God's sheep, a dead lion, a dead bear. Maybe tally marks next to each dead animal? It should come as no surprise then, that before David heads to the battlefield, he would grab his staff. Thus, strengthening himself in his triumphs and giving testimony to remember God's covenant promise with him. Remember, 'testimony' comes from a word that means 'to do again.' When David grabs his staff, he releases into the atmosphere a power for his victories to be done again.

I think it is worth pointing out that David didn't grab his rod before he faced Goliath. We know rods were what shepherds used to fight off predators. Instead, David grabbed his staff. The instrument used to lead and rescue. The instrument that highlighted for him his historical testimony of God's faithfulness as well as the history of who he is. Somehow David knew strength wouldn't win this battle, but covenant would. When David grabbed his staff, strengthening himself in the Lord, he was prophesying Goliath's future.

We know David is from the tribe of Judah, which we often associate with meaning 'praise.' 'Judah' is derived from the Hebrew word '*yadah*,' which means 'to extend the hand.' I like how Dutch Sheets explains it: "Because Judah means 'to extend the hand,' it can also mean 'to throw a stone.' He becomes proficient at throwing stones because, 'that's who I am in my DNA, in my history. I am from the tribe that throws stones (extends the hand).' When David faced the giant, all he did was tap into his historical, God-given DNA."[6]

In fact, David was so proficient at being Judah (*yadah*), the Bible says when he slung the stone, it sank into Goliath's forehead. '*Taba*' is the word here used for 'sank,' and it also means 'to be drowned.' David slung that stone with so much force, it submerged itself into Goliath's forehead, never to be seen again.

Just like the Shunammite- David had a promise from God. He was from the tribe of Judah. This was his land. His promise from God, and now his promise was being tested by a giant uncircumcised Philistine. When you face a giant, sling the staff of your testimony in its face with so much force, you lodge it permanently into the giant's head, forcing your destiny to now become his reality.

David was a man after God's heart. David's name means 'beloved.' David was victorious because he focused on God's love for him. When David went up against Goliath, he was relying on God's unfailing love to lead him into victory. The covenant promises of God are everlasting. We must align ourselves with them by decreeing, as David did, that every other kingdom is coming to an end.

We partner with heaven when we decree that God's Kingdom is established in the earth, enduring forever. The Lord is zealously faithful to uphold His covenant, as we see in Psalm 89:34: "My covenant I will not break, nor alter the thing that is gone out of my lips."

He promises to never alter it; He is God, and He does not change. It's time to start decreeing our covenant promises; to see darkness flee and light bear forth on the earth. "When the enemy comes in like a flood, the Spirit of the Lord will lift up a standard against him. The Redeemer will come to Zion" (Isaiah 59:19-20; NKJV).

Now that we clearly understand David's DNA, we need to look at the purpose behind Goliath's. Goliath's name is derived from the word *'galah'* and means 'to uncover, remove, display, or reveal.' It appears from this, that Goliath's destiny was to reveal and display, or in this case, draw forth, David's destiny. Goliath's presence brought forth the secret life of David.

Goliath validated David's staff, opening the eyes wide of everyone in David's life. In fact, one of the explanations for Goliath's name paints a picture of a human agent used by God to reveal secrets. With one stone, David's entire staff was solidified, declaring who he really was, and confirming God's covenant promises with him.

We read in 1 Samuel 17:23 that Goliath is the champion of Gath. Gath is a Philistine city, and the name 'Gath' means 'wine press.'[7] A wine press is a mechanism used to extract fruit juice from crushed grapes. It accomplishes this by exerting controlled pressure onto the fruit. The process necessitates that the pressure be controlled in order to prevent crushing the seeds, which would produce a great deal of unwanted tannins into the wine.

Is this not the very thing Goliath was doing? Goliath was exerting controlled pressure on Israel, thereby extracting, or drawing out, David and the fruit in David's life to the frontline of the battle. If Goliath had not exerted this pressure on Israel, we would not have known David as we do.

While some tannins add flavor, too much, or the wrong kind, can turn the whole batch bitter and astringent. Tannins are the primary determinant of the longevity of red wines. Winemakers can decipher what stage the wine's development is in, as well as its potential for aging, based on the character of the tannins.

Steven Thompson, the founder of Analemma wines, says, "tannins are in some way the bones of the wine- the skeleton. They give structure and are what carries a wine for a long way in the cellar and the bottle."[8]

If we look at this biblically, we can see that God takes advantage of the giants in your life. He uses them to draw you out, to reveal your DNA, and to solidify His covenant promises with you, and your destiny with Him. All of this is meant to extract fruit from your life and establish structure, which is intended to produce new wine.

Sometimes God will put a Goliath in your life to draw out the David within you. Don't allow that process to turn you into bitter, harsh wine. Instead, grab your staff, press into your promises, and lay hold of your destiny. Battles are not about circumstances. Battles are about trust, and trust is built on covenant.

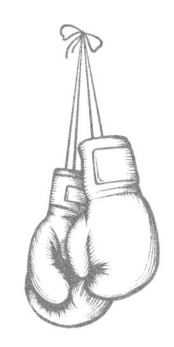

WHOLEHEARTED
Trusting In Your Promise

The second year after the Exodus from Egypt, the Lord instructed Moses to send some men to explore the land of Canaan, which the Lord was intending to give to the Israelites. He tells Moses to send one leader from each of the twelve tribes to spy out the land and report back. Moses obeys.

Moses instructs the twelve spies to fully explore the area and see what the land is like- the people, the soil, the vegetation, all of it. He also tells them to bring back some fruit of the land. We learn from Numbers 13:23, they cut off a branch bearing a single cluster of grapes. It was so large, two men carried it on a pole between them, along with some pomegranates and figs. Hello, abundance.

After exploring the land for forty days, they returned. "They gave Moses this account: "We went into the land to which you sent us, and it does flow with milk and honey! Here is its fruit. But the people who live there are powerful, and the cities are fortified and very large. We even saw descendants of Anak there" (Numbers 13:27-29; NIV).

The Anak were giants. Goliath was a descendant from this race. Bible Study Tools says this about them: "Their formidable warlike appearance, as described by the spies sent to search the land, filled the Israelites with terror."[9]

Caleb represented the prince of Judah and he was the leader of this tribe, sent out as a spy. He interrupts the fear and silences everyone. He gives a much different report in verse 30, instructing Moses, "We should go up and take possession of the land, for we can certainly do it."

In other words, Caleb understands that the Lord is on their side and they have the promise of the Lord. This is their inheritance, their land. Therefore, it doesn't matter how big the giants are or how many giants there are, the Israelites will taste victory because the battle is the Lord's, and they hold His covenant promise.

None of the other spies will listen to Caleb though, except Joshua. The ten other spies proclaim they can't attack the giants because the giants are stronger. They spread word throughout all the Israelites a bad report about the land the Lord had intended to give them. They spread fear like wildfire in the hearts of all the men, causing them to tremble at the giants, instead of fearing the Lord.

"…The land we explored devours those living in it. All the people we saw there are of great size. We saw the Nephilim there (the descendants of Anak come from the Nephilim). We seemed like grasshoppers in our own eyes, and we looked the same to them" (Numbers 13:32-33).

The Israelites were so filled with fear, they started grumbling and crying out, declaring they wished they had stayed in Egypt. They assumed the Lord was bringing them to this land only for them to be slaughtered. They started discussing with each other about choosing a new leader for themselves and heading back to Egypt. They were ready to completely abandon the Lord's promise to them because it didn't look the way they thought it should. It didn't happen the way they expected.

Joshua and Caleb responded to this by declaring, "The land we passed through and explored is exceedingly good. If the Lord is pleased with us, He will lead us into that land, a land flowing with milk and honey, and will give it to us. Only do not rebel against the Lord. And do not be afraid of the people of the land, because we will devour them. Their protection is gone, but the Lord is with us. Do not be afraid of them" (Numbers 14:7-9; NIV).

This did nothing to persuade the Israelites, who were now intending to stone Caleb and Joshua. At this, the glory of the Lord appeared to all the Israelites.

"The Lord said to Moses, 'How long will these people treat me with contempt? How long will they refuse to believe in me, in spite of all the signs I have performed among them? I will strike them down with a plague and destroy them, but I will make you into a nation greater and stronger than they" (Numbers 14: 11-12; NIV).

The Lord was testing Moses' heart. Moses tells the Lord this is a bad idea. He reasons, everyone knows the Lord delivered the Israelites, and if He kills them now, word will spread to the surrounding nations the Lord wasn't able to keep His promise to them, so He slaughtered them in the wilderness. Moses reminds the Lord that He is abounding in love and forgiveness and appeals to the Lord to forgive them. He also reminds the Lord that he does not leave the guilty unpunished, but He punishes the children for the sin of the parents- to the third and fourth generation.

The Lord decides to forgive them, but it will not go unpunished. Not one of the people who treated the Lord with contempt will see the promised land. Verse 24 says, "But because my servant Caleb has a different spirit and follows me wholeheartedly, I will bring him into the land he went to, and his descendants will inherit it." Interestingly, the name 'Caleb' means 'wholehearted.' Caleb, walking fully in who God had made Him to be- honored the Lord.

"Lord, who dares to dwell with you? Who presumes the privilege of being close to you, living next to you in your shining place of glory? Who are those who daily dwell in the life of the Holy Spirit? They are passionate and wholehearted, always sincere and always speaking the truth- for their hearts are trustworthy" (Psalm 15:1-2; TPT).

The Lord declared that because the Israelites had grumbled, He would do to them the very thing He heard them say, and in the wilderness their bodies would fall. Every person who was twenty years of age or older who grumbled would not enter the promised land. An entire generation missed their blessing, their promise, their covenant, their life. All because they didn't count the Lord faithful. All because they thought their giants were bigger than their God.

"Your children will be shepherds here for forty years, suffering for your unfaithfulness, until the last of your bodies lies in the wilderness. For forty years – one year for each of the forty days you explored the land – you will suffer for your sins and know what it is like to have me against you" (Numbers 14:33-34; NIV).

So, the ten spies who gave the bad report were struck down with a plague and died. This turned all the Israelites bitter. Early the next morning they planned to charge forth and take their promised land despite what the Lord had said. Moses tried to stop them, asking them why they were disobeying the Lord. Their disobedience would not succeed because the Lord was not with them. Because they had turned away from the Lord, He would not be with them in battle, and they would fall by the sword. They didn't listen and they went on ahead without Moses and without the Ark of the Lord's Covenant.

The Amalekites and the Canaanites rose up and attacked them and routed them to the town of Hormah. 'Hormah' means 'devotion.' Joshua would eventually conquer Hormah. Joshua's name means 'Jehovah is salvation.' 'Israel' means 'God prevails.' Somehow, in the midst of fear, the Israelites had forgotten all this. They forgot who they were. And they forgot whose they were.

What can we learn from this? The ten spies thought it was important to report about all the obstacles they assumed the giants in the land would be, as they currently occupied their promise. They were looking at their promise without the Lord. Caleb thought it was best to only report on the milk and honey of Canaan, completely ignoring the giants in the land- only saying they would be as bread, a mere snack. Caleb was looking at His promise with the Lord. Caleb saw God as supreme and the giants as inconsequential. Once you see God in any situation, the enemy will always appear smaller.

We need to put our trust in the Lord, like Caleb did. We have no reason not to. In fact, we are promised blessing and protection when we do. Psalm 91 says:

> "When you sit enthroned under the shadow of Shaddai, you are hidden in the strength of God Most High. He's the hope that holds me and the stronghold to shelter me, the only God for me, and my great confidence. He will rescue you from every hidden trap of the enemy, and he will protect you from false accusation and any deadly curse. His massive arms are wrapped around you, protecting you. You can run under his covering of majesty and hide. His arms of faithfulness are a shield keeping you from harm. You will never worry about an attack of demonic forces at night nor have to fear a spirit of darkness coming against you. Don't fear a thing! Whether by night or by day, demonic danger will not trouble you, nor will the powers of evil launched against you. Even in a time of disaster, with thousands and thousands being killed, you will remain unscathed and unharmed. You will be a spectator as the wicked perish in judgment, for they will be paid back for what they have done! When we live our lives within the shadow of God Most High, our secret hiding place, we will always be shielded from harm. How then could evil prevail against us or disease infect us? God sends angels with special orders to protect you wherever you go, defending you from all harm. If you walk into a trap, they'll be there for you and keep you from stumbling. You'll even walk unharmed among the fiercest powers of darkness,

trampling every one of them beneath your feet! For here is what the Lord has spoken to me: "Because you have delighted in me as my great lover, I will greatly protect you. I will set you in a high place, safe and secure before my face. I will answer your cry for help every time you pray, and you will find and feel my presence even in your time of pressure and trouble. I will be your glorious hero and give you a feast. You will be satisfied with a full life and with all that I do for you. For you will enjoy the fullness of my salvation" (TPT)!

This passage tells us that when we sit as one enthroned, as royalty with Christ, then we are hidden in His strength. Verse 4 tells us we find shelter under His wings. This is a reference to His angelic host and points us back to the Ark of Covenant, where His cherubim guarded over the mercy seat. His mercy seat has a 24/7, 365 day a year open door policy; always ready to welcome us when we need it without any fear He will reject or condemn us.

Verses 5 and 6 speak of not only being protected against natural forces of evil, but also being protected against spiritual forces of evil. When we live in and from our secret place, in God, we are protected on every side and from every force evil. He governs His angels to protect us wherever we go. When we delight in Him, He takes care of the rest.

This is our inheritance in the Lord. This is the war cry over our lives. When we live in Him, we have no need. When we live in Him, we have no threat. When we live in Him, we have only assurance. Truly, there is only good news.

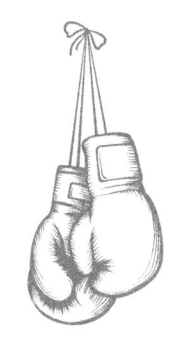

CAPTAIN OF THE HOSTS OF THE LORD
Your Promise Is A Roadmap

After Moses dies, the Lord instructs Joshua to cross over into the Promised Land. The Lord tells Joshua three times in chapter one to 'be strong and courageous,' as Joshua is going to fulfill the Lord's promise to this generation of people. Joshua prepares the mighty men of valor, while also secretly sending in two spies to inspect the land. The spies enter the house of Rahab- the least likely place the enemy would suspect to find the children of God. The Bible tells us she is a prostitute, but she also has faith in God.

Word travels to the king of Jericho that Rahab is housing two spies. He tells Rahab to bring the men to him, but she hid them instead. She lies to the king and tells him she doesn't know who the men are, but she thinks she saw them leave as the city gate was closing. In reality, she hid them on her roof.

After the king leaves, Rahab checks on the spies and says, "I know that the Lord has given you this land and that the fear of you has fallen on us, so that all who dwell in the land are melting in fear of you. For we have heard how the Lord dried up the waters of the Red Sea before you when you came out of Egypt, and what you did to Sihon and Og, the two kings of the Amorites across the Jordan, whom you devoted to destruction. When we heard this, our hearts melted and everyone's courage failed because of you, for the Lord your God is

God in the heavens above and on the earth below" (Joshua 2:8-11; Berean Study Bible).

She gives a tremendous account of the testimony of their victories echoed throughout the land, and it has fully intimidated the enemy. Next, she strikes an agreement with the spies, asking for them to show kindness to her and her family, and in exchange, she will continue to help them. They agree and decide to use a scarlet cord (ribbon) as a symbol of their agreement, visibly displayed in her window.

The spies make it back to Joshua and report, "'The Lord has surely delivered the entire land into our hands,' they said to Joshua. 'Indeed, all who dwell in the land are melting in fear of us'" (Joshua 2:24; Berean Study Bible).

The next morning, the Israelites move to the Jordan, where they will camp before they cross over. After three days of camping, the officers move through the camp, commanding everyone to follow the Ark of the Covenant of the Lord. Then Joshua tells the people in verse 5 to, "consecrate yourselves, for tomorrow the Lord will do wonders among you."

As a sign to the people that the Lord was still with them, the Lord tells Joshua to select a leader from each of the twelve tribes of Israel to carry the Ark to the Jordan. He promises that as they do, He will part the water, and they will cross on dry ground. The entire nation, 40,000 troops who are armed for battle, cross over.

The Lord then instructs Joshua to choose a man from each of the twelve tribes. He commands them to pick twelve stones from the middle of the Jordan, where the priests were standing, carry them, and set them down where they will spend the night. Joshua obeys and informs the twelve men to carry the stones on their shoulders. He tells them the stones will serve as a memorial to the Israelites of what the Lord has done for them this day.

They make it to Gilgal to set up camp and Joshua sets up the twelve stones they took from the Jordan. Joshua tells the Israelites the stones are a memorial for future generations, to remember what the Lord has done- a sign of their covenant with Him.

"He did this so that all the peoples of the earth may know that the hand of the Lord is mighty, and so that you may always fear the Lord your God" (Joshua 4:24; Berean Study Bible).

When word travels to the Amorite and Canaanite kings about what the Lord has done, the Bible says in verse 1 of chapter 5, "their hearts melted and their spirits failed for fear of the Israelites."

The Lord commands Joshua to make flint knives and circumcise the sons of Israel. This was necessary because all the men who came out of Egypt died in the wilderness, because they did not obey the Lord. So, He raised up their sons in their place, but none of the men who were born in the wilderness had been circumcised yet. Before they can enter their Promised Land, all the men of Israel need to be circumcised and consecrated to the Lord.

From a military standpoint, immediately striking the enemy after they had crossed over, would make logical sense. The men were charged with excitement over just witnessing the miraculous parting of the waters and the enemy was literally melting with fear. This is not how the Lord's kingdom economy works though.

For God, spiritual values, priorities, and principles are far more vital and fundamental to victory. In our modern culture especially, we are always in a hurry to get things moving. But to be victorious from God's standpoint, certain things will be vital if we are going to attack the fortresses in this life with His strength, and according to His principles.

Before Israel could be ready to advance on Jericho, their hearts needed to be prepared. Their willingness to submit to God's leading, so they could experience His power, needed to be fully established. We can glean from this story that they followed five steps of consecration before the Lord told them they were ready to advance. Let's unpack them.

First (5:1), they received a report about the morale of the inhabitants of their Promised Land. For us, it is imperative to spiritual victory that we understand who we are in Christ. All the enemies we face today are melting with fear because they have already been defeated through Christ (Rom 6; Colossians 2:1-15; Hebrews 2:14). The enemy is terrified of YOU. Terrified you will come to a revelation of the authority you have over him, through King Jesus.

Second (5:2-9), their covenant needed to be renewed with the Lord. The men born in the wilderness needed to be circumcised as Moses' generation was. This was a covenant the Lord made with Abraham and represented Israel's faith in God's ability to hold His promise true. In this case, part of the promise of the covenant included the possession of the Promised Land, as their inheritance. We previously discussed in the Back to Bedrock chapter that Jesus is our New Testament model for the Ark of the Covenant.

Third (5:10), they participated in the Passover, and relived their deliverance out of Egypt by the blood of the Lamb. This was also related to their Promised Land. They observed the Passover in Egypt and the destroying angel passed over their house, ultimately leading them to the crossing of the Red Sea, which led to the defeat of the Egyptians. Likewise, crossing the Jordan would be followed by the defeat of the Canaanites. We have previously discussed, 'the testimony of Jesus is the spirit of prophecy,' from Revelations 19:10. This story is an old testament model of that spiritual truth. They were giving testimony to God's past faithfulness to them, impregnating their atmosphere with faith to believe for His victory to be manifest again in their situation

Fourth (5:11-12), the manna ceased, and they began to eat the produce of their Promised Land. Deliverance from Egypt included the promise they would inherit the land, a land of abundance- wheat, barley, fig trees, olive oil, and honey. It was a sign of new life and new beginnings. They had been delivered from judgement and were rock solid (the twelve stones) in the place of blessing. Eating the fruit of their promise was a prophetic declaration- giving the enemy notice, if you will.

Bible.org says, "The Passover not only looked back, but it looked forward to their new life in the land enjoying its abundant blessings by the power of God, and so eating of the produce was an act of confirmation of God's abundant blessing."[10]

Fifth (5:13-15), Joshua encounters the Captain of the Hosts of the Lord. Joshua needed an encounter with the Lord. He was surveying the land of Jericho, no doubt feeling overwhelmed at trying to formulate a battle plan against an incredibly fortified city, as their own weaponry was seriously insufficient. As he is doing this, he encounters the Lord, standing opposite him, with a sword drawn.

"Standing with any weapon drawn is a military position of one who either stands guard or who stands ready to go against a foe defensively or offensively. Standing with sword drawn suggested He was there to fight either against, or with, or for Israel" (Bible.org).

Joshua asks Him if He is there for the Israelites or for the enemy. He doesn't know yet that it's preincarnate Jesus. So, it's a logical question. None of Israel's army has been given instruction to fight yet, but here stands a man, facing Joshua with His sword drawn.

Preincarnate Jesus responds, 'neither.' He then gives Joshua the battle plan, and it looks nothing like Joshua expected it would. Typical. God has an incredible knack for seemingly unconquerable circumstances and unconventional tactics.

This encounter is incredibly significant and highlights for us a typical mindset we often fall prey to. We tend to see battles we are in as belonging to us or being our full responsibility. And we see those in the enemy's camp as our enemies; whether through different agendas, different political affiliations, theologies, doctrines, campaigns, etc. But the Lord says He is on no one's side.

"The Lord is not slow about His promise, as some count slowness, but is patient toward you, not wishing for any to perish but for all to come to repentance" (2 Peter 3:9).

We see this a lot in the Body of Christ, where we assume because we are Christians, the Lord is on our side. But with respect to humanity, He loves all His children, whether they are walking with Him or not. We do not war against flesh and blood. We can currently see this today as you can't turn on the news without hearing about impeachment- the ongoing war between democrats and republicans. God is not a democrat or a republican.

God is on the side of His plans, purposes, covenants, and promises- and these things have everything to do with His passionate love and His passionate lovers. "But just look at them now, in panic, trembling with terror. For the Lord is on the side of the generation of loyal lovers" (Psalm 14:5; TPT).

As human beings, we can either choose to be loyal lovers, on God's side, or be in the way. Rahab was not an Israelite, and even though she was walking in great darkness and sin, her life was sparred because she believed in God and aligned with His plans and purposes. The same is true today.

Until this point in the story, the inhabitants of Jericho have been melting in fear. They could have fled or surrendered, they could have partnered with God's plans like Rahab did, but they chose to remain locked-in. Those that stood in the way of God's agenda, were destroyed.

The Lord is appearing to him as the Captain of the Hosts of the Lord, to give Joshua the battle plan. Why? Because God is jealous about covenant. So, Jesus as the Captain of the Hosts of the Lord, is on the scene to take charge as the Commander of the Lord's army. The Lord shows up with the armies of heaven to secure Jericho so God's people can possess their God-given inheritance, their Promised Land.

The Lord will be shown faithful to His promise. When we submit to His leadership, then the battle truly belongs to Him.

Proverbs 3:5-10 says, "Trust in the Lord completely, and do not rely on your own opinions. With all your heart rely on him to guide you, and he will lead you in every decision you make. Become intimate with him in whatever you do, and he will lead you wherever you go. Don't think for a moment that you know it all, for wisdom comes when you adore him with undivided devotion and avoid everything that's wrong. Then you will find the healing refreshment your body and spirit long for. Glorify God with all your wealth, honoring him with your very best, with every increase that comes to you. Then every dimension of your life will overflow with blessings from an uncontainable source of inner joy" (TPT)!

Joshua beautifully responds to the Captain of the Hosts of Lord by falling on his face and asking, "What has my Lord to say to his servant" (Joshua 5:14)?

Joshua was submitting to his Commander for orders through worship and submission, and the Lord faithfully delivered. It is a wonderful reminder to us of God promising His presence and His provision. Jesus tells Joshua to remove his sandals because he is standing on holy ground. This act was a symbol of servanthood, respect, and submission.

Bible.org says, "God is not only the Holy One in our redemption through the provision of the suffering Savior, but He is the Holy One in our warfare through the Victorious Savior. We can only enter into the battle so that we experience God's deliverance when we remove our sandals and submit to His authority and His presence and power."[11]

Jesus tells Joshua they are to march around Jericho once, for six consecutive days with seven priests carrying seven trumpets of rams' horns in front of the Ark. On the seventh day, they are to march around the city seven times. On the last march around the city, the priests are to blow the horns while everyone shouts. When they do this, the city walls will fall down.

"And it was so, that when Joshua had spoken to the people, the seven priests carrying the seven trumpets of rams' horns before the LORD went forward and blew the trumpets; and the Ark of the Covenant of the LORD followed them. The armed men went before the priests who blew the trumpets, and the rear guard came after the

Ark, while they continued to blow the trumpets. But Joshua commanded the people, saying, "You shall not shout nor let your voice be heard nor let a word proceed out of your mouth, until the day I tell you, 'Shout!' Then you shall shout!" So he had the Ark of the Lord taken around the city, circling it once; then they came into the camp and spent the night in the camp" (Joshua 6:8-11).

They did this for six days. On the seventh day, they marched around the city seven times. At the seventh time, when the priests blew their trumpets, Joshua told the people, "Shout! For the Lord has given you the city. The city shall be under the ban, it and all that is in it belongs to the Lord; only Rahab the harlot and all who are with her in the house shall live, because she hid the messengers whom we sent" (Joshua 6:16-17).

They did as he commanded, and the wall fell flat. They destroyed the inhabitants in the city and burned the entire place to the ground, never to be rebuilt again.

I was reflecting on the 'shout' and the trumpets blowing, wondering what was significant about this. It reminded me of how Gideon and his 300 men defeated an army without number, by blowing trumpets, breaking pots, and shouting: "A sword for the Lord and for Gideon!" The entire army of the enemy fled from Gideon in fear. Two stories in the Bible where the victories were won by lots of noise and shouting. As I thought about what could be significant about this, I remembered a teaching I heard from Dutch Sheets about air supremacy. He introduces the topic by sharing about a tactic the Israeli army employed in 1967.

In the first half of 1967, Egypt and other Arab nations surrounding Israel began making hostile moves against the vastly outnumbered Israeli military. Their aggressive moves reached a head in June 1967 when the Egyptian, Syrian, and Jordanian militaries looked ready to swarm Israel and overpower it.

In response, on June 5, 1967, Israel launched a multitude of pre-emptive airstrikes, virtually destroying the entire powerful

Egyptian air force and giving Israel air supremacy. With air supremacy established, the much smaller Israeli military soundly defeated the larger militaries of the opposing nations, killing over 20,000 troops while only losing fewer than 1,000 of its own, and taking new territory from Israel's enemies.

"As God demonstrated through Israel, air supremacy is a key to victory. There's a difference between air superiority and air supremacy, terms often used synonymously. Air supremacy is the top position in air control in war, where a side holds complete control of air warfare and air power over opposing forces. It is defined by NATO as the opposing air force being incapable of effective interference throughout the entire war. Air supremacy means one side holds total domination over the other. Air superiority is the second level, below air supremacy, where one side is in a more favorable position than the opponent, but not domination."[12]

As believers in Christ, our territory, or atmosphere to conquer, will occur through the vehicle of prayer. We will shout as Joshua did, and gain air supremacy as Israel did, when we engage as the interceding movement of Christ.

"God has given us air supremacy and we are now no longer only going to move in the priestly aspect of intercession, we are going to marry it with the kingly aspect of intercession. We are not just priests who offer up petitions, we are not just a priesthood that worships, we are not just priests that go and ask and represent planet earth to Him, we are now moving into the royal priesthood area. The Melchizedek order of kings and priests. A Kingdom of priests where we represent the King from up there, seated with Him, and we are not just going to ask as priests, we are going to decree as kings. (No longer praying like a widow, but a bride). We are going to make our decrees and where we have been quoting, 'You will decree a thing and it will be established,' we are going to do more than quote it now. We are going to decree a thing and we are going to watch the situation change" (Dutch Sheets).

As I dug into the word, I found that 'shouting' is referenced a lot in the Bible. It almost always seems to be accompanied with battle, victory in battle, salvation, or proclamation. The battle of David and Goliath was precipitated with forty days of shouting. Forty days of neither army able to gain air supremacy. Forty days of Goliaths' shout going uncontested until David arrived on the scene and shouted back.

We can learn from this that they were jockeying for air supremacy. We know David was a youth and Goliath was a giant. There is likely no way David could have shouted louder than Goliath. This should teach us that the path to air supremacy then, is not about how loud you shout, but more importantly, it is about what you say.

If you recall, David said, "You come against me with sword and spear and javelin, but I come against you in the name of the Lord Almighty, the God of the armies of Israel, whom you have defied. This day the Lord will deliver you into my hands, and I'll strike you down and cut off your head…All those gathered here will know that it is not by sword or spear that the Lord saves; for the battle is the Lord's, and he will give all of you into our hands" (1 Samuel 17:45-47; NIV).

All David did was announce that because he was in covenant with the Lord and Goliath was not, the Lord would cause David to be victorious. In fact, if you'll notice throughout the entire story, David never calls Goliath by name. He only ever calls him the 'uncircumcised Philistine.' He only ever addresses Goliath as the one who is not in covenant with God.

War cries have long been used to arouse and rally people to a cause or battle. They are also meant as a weapon of intimidation against an enemy. Most commonly though, we see them in the Bible as a symbol of victory. In fact, David says in Psalm 41:11, "By this I know that You are pleased with me, because my enemy does not shout in triumph over me."

Isaiah 42:13 is perhaps the best passage I see this reference played out, "The Lord will march forth like a mighty hero; He will come out like a warrior, full of fury. He will shout his battle cry and crush all his enemies" (NLT).

We need to transition our thinking from a hand-to-hand combat mentality with the enemy, to an air strike mentality. We need to address battle as royalty, seated with Christ.

Caleb taught us it doesn't matter how big the giants are, God can defeat them. David taught us it doesn't matter how small we are, God will cause us to be victorious.

"The Lord is their strength, and He is a saving defense to His anointed" (Psalm 28:8).

When we realize just how faithful He is, our entire mindset can change. It's not that the enemy isn't present anymore, it's that the enemy doesn't matter anymore. We can take God at His word. Battles are not about circumstances. Battles are about trust, and trust is built on covenant. When we stand on His promises, we advance in His purposes.

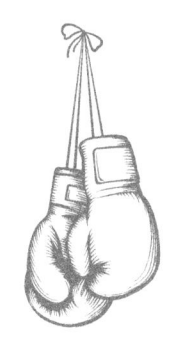

THE LION'S SHARE
Unleashing The Roar Of Heaven

Jesus was born in Bethlehem, a city of David. 'Bethlehem' means 'house of bread'. One of the names for Jesus is 'The Bread of Life.' This comes from a verse in John 6:32: "'The truth is,' Jesus said, 'Moses didn't give you the bread of heaven. It's my Father who offers bread that comes as a dramatic sign from heaven. The bread of God is the One who came out of heaven to give his life to feed the world'" (TPT).

The Passion Translation footnote in reference to 'a dramatic sign' reads, "The Aramaic can be translated 'a rainbow sign.' Just as Noah was given a rainbow sign of the covenant God was making with him, Jesus' earthly life was a rainbow sign from heaven of the new covenant life given to every believer today."

As we learned from the chapter on David and Goliath, one of the definitions for 'Judah' (*yadah*), is to 'extend the hand.' David being from Judah, extended the stone in his hand to take down Goliath and lay hold of his promise.

Jesus is referred to as 'The Lion of the Tribe of Judah (*yadah*).' **He extended both His hands** on the cross to defeat Satan, laying hold of the promise of His bride. The word '*yadah*' is made from three Hebrew letters: '*hei*,' '*dalet*,' and '*yud*.' '*Hei*' means '**grace**,' '*dalet*' means '**door**,' and '*yud*' means '**hand**.' Hebrew is read from right to left. So, when we speak of '*yadah*,' what we are giving testimony to is this: Jesus extended His hands on the cross, opening forever a door for grace.

"but we speak God's wisdom in a mystery, the hidden wisdom which God predestined before the ages to our glory; the wisdom which none of the rulers of this age has understood; for if they had understood it they would not have crucified the Lord of glory" (1 Corinthians 2:7-8).

Jesus is called the 'Son of David' because he is a descendant from the line of David. Two kings, same tribe, both slaying giants by extending their hands. Both walking in covenant promises with God. Both tapping into their inheritance to slay the giants before them. Both modeling for us the power of covenant, historical testimony, and DNA. And I would propose to you that Jesus extended his hands with more vigor than David flung the stone.

The word used for 'staff' in 1 Samuel 17 is the word '*maqqel*' or '*maqqelah.*' Interestingly, one of the definitions given for '*maqqlah*' is from an unused root meaning apparently 'to germinate.'[13] Germination is what happens when a seed begins to grow and develop. When a seed germinates, it produces a shoot.

We read in Isaiah, "Then a shoot will spring up from the stump of Jesse, and a Branch from his roots will bear fruit…On that day the Root of Jesse will stand as a banner for the peoples. The nations will seek Him, and His place of rest will be glorious. On that day the Lord will **extend His hand** a second time to recover the remnant of His people…He will raise a banner for the nations and gather the exiles of Israel; He will collect the scattered of Judah… There will be a highway for the remnant of His people" (Isaiah 11:1,10-11, 12, 16; Berean Study Bible).

Jesus being the Lion of Judah, extended both his hands on the cross to take down Satan. Isaiah 11 tells us He will do it a second time, at His return, to recover the remnant- though this time it will not be on a cross.

Goliath could not recognize the anointing on David because Goliath was blinded by the pride of his own stature. Likewise, Satan could not recognize the power of love as Jesus approached crucifixion because Satan only loves himself. Both giants were blindsided. Goliath could only see a child and not Judah. Satan could only see a Lamb headed to slaughter and not the Lion of the Tribe of Judah. Goliath could only see a boy and not a king. Satan could only see a man with a death sentence and not the King of Kings.

"I, Jesus, have sent my angel to give you this testimony for the churches. I am the Root and Offspring of David, and the bright Morning Star" (Revelation 22:16; NIV).

As we learned from David and Goliath, being in covenant relationship with God is a powerful weapon in battle. In battle we are meant to stand on our covenant promises, the anchor of our souls, as we read in Hebrews 6:19-20: "This hope we have as an anchor of the soul, a hope both sure and steadfast and one which enters within the veil, where Jesus has entered as a forerunner for us, having become a high priest forever according to the order of Melchizedek."

The name 'Melchizedek' means 'king of justice or righteousness.' Genesis 14 introduces us to Melchizedek as the king of Salem. 'Salem' means 'peace.' Salem is also an early name for Jerusalem. God's law specified that only those born of the tribe of Levi could serve as His priests (Numbers 8), and even then, only those who descended from Aaron were eligible to become high priests.

Jesus is from the tribe of Judah, which means He would not be eligible under the law to be a high priest. In God's wisdom, He intended for the Old Covenant Levitical priesthood to be temporary. The biblical appearance of Melchizedek occurred may decades before Levi, and more than 300 years before Israel received the law (Exodus 20). The existence of Melchizedek meant that Jesus would not be bound by its rules regarding priesthood.

Hebrews 7 tells us the High Priest of Melchizedek has no beginning and no end. He has an unlimited life of resurrection power. He is able to save and rescue, for all time and eternity. He is a new covenant, sealed with the oath of God. He is enthroned at the right of God and is our High Priest forever.

"Now this is the crowning point of what we are saying: we have a magnificent King-Priest who ministers for us at the right hand of God. He is enthroned with honor next to the throne of the Majesty on high. He serves in the holy sanctuary in the true heavenly tabernacle set up by God, and not by men" (Hebrews 8:1-2; TPT).

Jesus entering within the veil has securely granted permanent access for us, for all time and eternity. He has made it possible for us to obtain our covenant promises, because He is our atonement. It is settled in Heaven and this cannot be undone by any force of evil.

Daniel 2:44 says, "In the days of those kings the God of heaven will set up a kingdom which will never be destroyed, and the kingdom will not be left for another people; it will crush and put an end to all these kingdoms, but it will itself endure forever."

This is now our testimony for us who believe, this is our hope and anchor. It covers our past, emboldens our present, and prophecies our future. Jesus is our King and He is our Great Shepherd. Colossians 2:15 tells us that when Jesus disarmed the rulers and authorities, He made a public display of them. "Having disarmed principalities and powers, He made a public spectacle of them, triumphing over them in it" (NKJV).

The root meaning of this passage in the Greek paints a picture of a victor who is so excessively triumphant, he parades his victory in open public, dragging his defeated prisoner behind him for everyone to see. We know from reading verse 50 of 1 Samuel 17, the stone David threw at Goliath killed him. Even still, verse 51 tells us David drew Goliath's sword from its sheath and cut his head off with it. This seemed odd to me until I dove deeper.

David dragged Goliath's head to Jerusalem. Jerusalem was not David's capital, but a place known for inhabiting God's enemies. The New Testament tells us that Christ was crucified at a spot outside Jerusalem called Golgotha. In Aramaic, 'Golgotha' means 'place of the skull.' The Latin word for 'skull' is *'calvaria,'* and in English, many Christians refer to the site of the crucifixion as Calvary.

We can glean from this a foreshadowing of Jesus Christ. David was declaring, perhaps even prophesying to God's enemies, essentially giving them notice; 'there will come a One who will **extend His hands** and slay the giant in this land and crush his head."

We see this promise in Genesis 3:15, at the first occurrence of sin, as God responds, "And I will put enmity between you and the woman, and between your offspring and hers; he (Jesus) will crush your head, and you (Satan) will strike his heel (crucify Him)" (NIV).

This is the first promise in scripture of a Redeemer. It tells us of the Promised One, coming from the seed of a woman, the virgin birth of Jesus Christ. Christ is called the 'Lion of the Tribe of Judah.' Lions are called 'kings of the jungle' because of their raw strength and power. Lions fear no other animal. However, the raw strength and power of Christ doesn't come through sheer physical force. It comes from His deep capacity to love, which fueled His sacrifice.

In most kingdoms, the establishment of authority is based on brute strength and power, or excessive wealth. The brute strength and power that defines Father's kingdom is based entirely on love. Love is the currency of Heaven. God himself is love, as we read in 1 John 4:8. This is what His kingdom is built on, and everything is governed through it.

As we discussed earlier, it was within Goliath's DNA to draw out, or reveal to us, David's DNA and destiny. Likewise, it was within Satan's DNA to draw out Christ. In fact 'Lucifer,' referred to as the 'morning star' and 'son of the dawn' in Isaiah 14:12, comes from the words '*shachar*' and '*helel*' which mean 'light bearer, dawn, son of the dawn, shining one, or star of the morning.'

It is interesting to me that what precipitated the battle with David and Goliath was Goliath's own arrogance. He was so sure of his status as a giant Philistine warrior, he thought himself undefeatable. It wasn't until he died that we understood who the actual mighty man of valor really was.

The same is true for Satan. The Bible tells us he was one of Heaven's most beautiful angels. His pride over his splendor led to his demise and ultimately drew out the true King of Glory. If Satan had never deceived Eve and led Adam to disobey, thereby introducing sin into the world, we would have never had need of a Redeemer.

Please understand, I am certainly not saying sin is justified so that we could have known Jesus as we do. I am simply saying God uses everything for good, and everything He does points to His goodness. He had a plan of redemption before He founded humanity. God is a promise keeper. When He enters into covenant with you, He is handing you a sword in the spirit with the enemy's name on it. Take up the sword of your covenant with Him and behead the enemy blocking your promise. It's time for the body of Christ to evict the enemy from Her land and own Her destiny.

We all long to see the manifested power of the Spirit in the earth; to see a great awakening reach the soil of men's hearts. We need to understand it is the crucifixion of Christ that fuels that power. There is no power if there is no crucifixion, and the crucifixion is nothing if it is not love. We need to so understand and identify with His crucifixion, that it becomes our only reality. Our very being needs to be branded by it.

In a general sense 'port of entry' is used to describe a place where someone can lawfully enter a country or territory. The port of entry grants them a legal right to enter the territory. This is exactly what Christ did for us. The crucifixion of Christ becomes a port of entry for us to not only obtain His victory for ourselves, but to also legislatively enforce it in the earth. We now have legal access because of Him.

In Revelation 19, John is caught up in Heaven and has just heard 'the thunderous voice of a great multitude' (19:6) shouting for joy as the Bride of Christ has made herself ready for the wedding celebration. The angel standing with John instructs him to write down the true words of God. John is so overwhelmed by the glory of what he is witnessing, he falls down at the angel's feet to worship him.

"Then I fell at his feet to worship him. But he said to me, "Do not do that; I am a fellow servant of yours and your brethren who hold the testimony of Jesus; worship God. For the testimony of Jesus is the spirit of prophecy" (Revelation 19:10).

The angel says something profound as he is rebuking John for worshipping him instead of God. He says that he is a fellow servant, like us, who holds the testimony of Jesus. Angels share with us the mission of carrying out God's will. With this, the angel is pointing us back to the Ark of the Covenant (Ark of the Testimony), with the cherubim overshadowing, or literally guarding over, God's holiness and will. He further adds that the testimony of Jesus is the spirit of prophecy. As we've discussed, the Old Testament reference for testimony is the Ten Commandments, and the New Testament reference for testimony is the finished work of the cross, and our history therein.

Looking at the original language for the last verse, we can better breakdown what the angel is saying to John. The word for 'testimony' in this verse comes from the original Greek word '*martyria*' and means 'to witness, evidence, testimony, reputation.' It comes from the original word '*martus*' meaning 'evidence given.' This is where we get the word 'martyr' from. With this we know that our testimony is empowered, literally only possible because of, the martyred death of Christ.

The word 'spirit' in this passage comes from the original word *'pneuma'* meaning 'wind, breath, spirit.' It is the Greek word equivalent in the New Testament, for the Old Testament Hebrew word, *'ruach,'* which is the Holy Spirit.

The words 'of prophecy' in this passage come from the original word *'propheteias,'* meaning 'prophecy, the gift of communicating and **enforcing revealed truth**.'

When you look at the original language for the last sentence of Revelation 19:10, taking into consideration each of the above word meanings, this verse can be said another way: "the testimonial witness of the death of Jesus Christ, causes to exist the spiritual enforcement of revealed truth, through the power of the Holy Spirit."

The Holy Spirit is the birthplace of prophecy and the principal focus of the revelation He provides, primarily points us to Jesus. Peter in fact indicates that all prophecy comes by the power of the Holy Spirit: "For no prophecy was ever made by an act of human will, but man moved by the Holy Spirit spoke from God" (2 Peter 1:21).

When God's prophets spoke in the Bible, it was God's Spirit speaking all the way through them. They were moved (*pneuma*) by the Holy Spirit. Speaking not their own desire but God's, which yielded their inspired testimony. They were essentially steered in prophetic utterance in like manner to a ship, driven by the wind, and subject to its force.

"And when the ship was caught in it and could not face the wind, we gave way to it and let ourselves be driven along" (Acts 27:15). The Aramaic uses the language, 'we surrendered to its power."

The power that once rested on the ark through the hovering presence of the Lord, now rests in us through the power of the Holy Spirit. When we testify of Jesus, the breath of the Spirit in us impregnates the atmosphere to enforce truth and literally declares

His light and truth into the atmosphere around us. It enforces air supremacy.

This is why it is so important to open our mouths, to obey the Holy Spirit, and give testimony of Jesus. It is the only true way to shift atmospheres, families, cities, and nations. We need to look at every circumstance through the lens of testimony. Giving testimony to the name of Jesus is fully, in and of itself, a complete prayer. Full stop. There is so much power in His name, when we speak it forth, our literal atmosphere shifts. Darkness trembles, veils fall, eyes open, and hearts awaken.

I remember a testimony from Smith Wigglesworth, sharing about a sick man who was bed ridden. Six people surrounded the sick man for prayer. The man was anointed, and they prayed James 5:14 over him but there was no immediate manifestation of healing. The sick man wept bitterly, and the six people left the room discouraged they had not seen a manifested healing. Then, something occurred to one of the six and he persuaded the others to go back into the room with him. He asked each of them to start whispering the name 'Jesus' with him.

Smith Wigglesworth shares this about what happened next; "At first when they whispered this worthy name nothing seemed to happen. But as they continued to whisper, "Jesus! Jesus! Jesus!" the power began to fall. As they saw that God was beginning to work, their faith and joy increased; and they whispered the name louder and louder. As they did so the man arose from his bed and dressed himself. The secret was just this, those six people had gotten their eye off the sick man, and they were just taken up with the Lord Jesus Himself, and their faith grasped the power that there is in His name. O, if people would only appreciate the power that there is in this name, there is no telling what would happen."

We need to stop staring at the enemy. We need to stop screaming at demons. We have been so distracted by what the devil is doing that we've relented all our power. We are grafted into the promises of God. Therefore, we too, are descendants of Judah. The tribe of Judah is full of giant slayers. Therefore, it's also in our spiritual DNA to slay giants. Because of the resurrection, our battleplan is to extend our hands heavenward. This is our greatest weapon. We need to pour out our hearts in pure worship. We need to wholeheartedly trust the Lord. We need to return to first love.

"But you are a chosen race, a royal priesthood, a holy nation, a people for God's own possession, so that you may proclaim the excellencies of Him who has called you out of darkness into His marvelous light; for you once were not a people, but now you are the people of God; you had not received mercy, but now you have received mercy" (1 Peter 2:9-10).

The power in His name carries so much weight, it transfuses darkness. "…I came that they may have life and have it abundantly" (John 10:10).

His testimony is now our testimony. We no longer live, but He lives in us. The Bible tells us in Revelation 12:10 that we overcome the enemy by the Blood of the Lamb and the word of our testimony, which is now the testimony of Christ. When we testify to that truth, we prophecy Christ's triumph into our reality. People often quote Ephesians 5:22 as proof a woman needs to submit to a man; but as The Passion Translation points out in the footnote, "The Greek word for "submit," or "supportive," is not found in v. 22." The original language reads: "Wives, with your husbands." For us to move forward as God's triumphant army, we need to understand His redemptive power and everything He paid the price for. We need to understand love is the currency of Heaven.

Battles are not about circumstances. Battles are about trust, and trust is built on covenant.

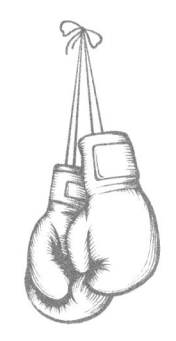

DEFINING EZER
Finding The Warrior Within

The battle for identity has never been greater. It is more important than ever we know who we are and whose we are. You were created for a unique purpose only you can fulfill. You are destined for victory and designed for greatness.

"Yet what honor you have given to men, created only a little lower than Elohim. Crowned like kings and queens with glory and magnificence. You have delegated to them mastery over all you have made, making everything subservient to their authority, placing earth itself under the feet of your image-bearers" (Psalm 8:4-6; TPT).

The Lord created us with purpose and intentionality. He created you to be a warrior, a bow in His quiver. We are destined to subdue the earth, to summon the Kingdom realm of our God into the earth. That we may stand as one with Him- 'on earth as it is in Heaven' (Matthew 6:10). We can't do this without knowing who we really are.

Genesis 2:18 reads, "Then the Lord God said, "It is not good for the man to be alone; I will make him a helper suitable for him."

I have historically always read this verse, and been taught, the role of a woman is to simply be subordinate to a man. We exist to meet their needs and help make their lives easier, by submitting to their every whim. We exist to be their assistants and servants in life, to compliantly do all they request of us- their 'help meet.' Anyone else struggled with this?

It wasn't until recently the Lord showed me what this passage is actually about. The Hebrew words used for 'helper suitable' are *'ezer kenegdo.'* The word *'ezer'* actually has two meanings in Hebrew: **'to rescue and save,'** and **'to be strong.'** Does that sound anything like a docile, subordinate assistant to you?

Ezer is actually a military term used 21 times in the Old Testament, twice to describe Eve (*Genesis 2:18; Genesis 2:20*), three times to describe Israel appealing to nations for military aid (*Isaiah 30:5; Ezekiel 12:14; Daniel 11:34*), and the remaining sixteen times the word is used to describe God himself as Israel's helper (*Exodus 18:4; Deuteronomy 33:7; Deuteronomy 33:26; Deuteronomy 33:29; Psalm 20:2; Psalm 33:20; Psalm 70:5; Psalm 89:19; Psalm 115:9; Psalm 115:10; Psalm 115:11; Psalm 121:1; Psalm 121:2; Psalm 124:8; Psalm 146:5; Hosea 13:9*).

What the above scriptures each have in common is they are used consistently in a military context. This makes is abundantly clear- *'ezer'* is a warrior, a mighty help in battle. God describes himself as *'ezer'* during times of war. The Psalmist refers to God as *'ezer'* when he says, "I lift up my eyes…where does my help come from" (Psalm 120)?

Ezer is made up of three Hebrew letters, reading from right to left: *ayin, zayin,* and *resh.* *'Ayin'* means **'eye,'** *'zayin'* means **'sword or armor,'** and *'resh'* means **'head of a man.'** Eve was created to provide valuable support and vital strength to Adam. He does the same thing for her. They have an equal partnership of corresponding strength and complementary power, dually made in His image.

When God made Eve, He made her an *'ezer,'* a warrior in times of need, a woman who could face the future with hope and courage. A woman of strength, might, and courage. An equal compliment to a man. Women were meant to be *'ezer's'* who imitate our Warrior King, and so are men. I am going to spend a bit more time unraveling this truth for women, as there is already a great deal of information available about what it means to be a mighty man of valor.

Finding The Warrior Within

I only just recently watched the movie Wonder Woman for the first time because I have been the busy mom of a two-year-old. While I am not interested in the mythology aspect of the film, the kindness, selfless love, and power of the leading lady stirred something deep inside me.

I am a little embarrassed to admit I watched the movie three times in a row, on the same day, crying my eyes out as I felt it awaken something inside of me. I felt it breath hope on an aspect of my identity and who God has made me to be. I felt it summoned something deep within me that hadn't been given life yet.

The director of the film, Patty Jenkins, shares this about the film, "The greatest thing about Wonder Woman is how good and kind and loving she is, yet none of that negates any of her power."

Women are known for being more emotional than men. In the film though, Wonder Woman's compassionate emotions serve as the catalyst that ignites her power. She is a beautiful combination of a sensitive woman and a fierce warrior, in one powerful package. I wept as I found myself empowered and emboldened as a woman of God. I felt I finally had permission to be fierce and vulnerable at the same time. I could suddenly see my vulnerabilities as a gift, as a weapon from God. I could see they were meant to make me stronger, not weaker.

In the film, everywhere Wonder Woman turns, she is told 'no, you can't do that.' As a child her mother tells her she can't learn to fight. As an adult her mother tells her she can't fight the humans' battle, she can't leave her home to help them, even though her mother knows this is her destiny. Her mother knows she was 'made' for this very thing, yet she still tries to limit her.

Captain Trevor constantly tell her, she's too distracting, she's not dressed right, she can't carry her armor around town, she can't be in meetings with men, she can't speak in the presence of men, she can't fight in the war, she can't go to the gala, she can't kill evil men, she doesn't know what she's talking about, and on and on.

She finally finds herself at the battlefield, where she always knew she was destined to be, at a place called 'No Man's Land.' The battalion has been there for months and hardly gained any progress. She wants to fight- to cross the other side and rescue the hostages. Again, she's told, 'no,' by Captain Trevor. She's told she can't fight here because both armies have been stuck here for months, neither side gaining an inch. He tells her she can't fight because it's a lost cause, a dead-end, a place without hope.

This time though, she doesn't listen. She is going to fight- and fight she does. She single-handedly wipes out the entire enemy army, which allows the soldiers to advance with force behind her. Then she advances to the village and rescues all the hostages. It was appropriately called 'no man's land,' as she, being a woman, fiercely forges ahead, paving the way for the army of men to advance behind her.

We can see another powerful testimony to the design of women from another Hollywood film. In the Lord of the Rings by J.R.R. Tolkien, the Nazgul were fallen spirits, in service to the Dark Lord. In the final battle of the movie, the king of the Nazgul is facing Eowyn, a shieldmaiden of Rohan. However, the Nazgul does not know she is a woman because she is completely covered in a man's battle armor.

As she is the only person standing between the Nazgul and his prey, the Nazgul warns her, "No man can kill me." At this, she takes off her helmet, revealing she is a woman, lifts her sword, and declares, "I am no man." And then she heroically drives her sword into his skull and kills him.

Eowyn was not previously allowed to fight in the battles of her people because she was a woman. She was confined to the traditional roles we often see for women. She finally decides she's had enough of the confinement, and chooses to defy oppression, eventually resulting in the death of the Nazgul king.

Now, I realize these are Hollywood films and not scripture. However, they beautifully define an aspect of womanhood that is sorely missing from the Body of Christ. As I have come to better understand God's design for woman, I wholeheartedly agree with Lou Engle when he says, "There are certain powers of darkness that can only be broken by women."[14]

"When we women stand firm in our God-given identity and calling, instead of heeding others' artificial labels, we can change the world…When her mission becomes her own and she is no longer bound by others' limitations or expectations. Then, she can be exactly who she was created to be" (Marilette Sanchez).[15]

As God's *ezer*, women have equal access, a port of entry if you will, to the promises and covenants of God. It is so imperative we have a clear understanding of God's intention for our lives. As Linda Heidler says: "No one, man or woman, can become who they were created to be until they have a clear picture of God's intention for them. If our belief system is skewed, then our identity will be skewed" (*The Apostolic Woman!*).

Deborah is one of the best biblical examples I have found in scripture of an *ezer* (Judges 4 and 5). She was a prophet of the Lord, a judge full of wisdom, a priestess, a leader, a worshipper, a poet, a songwriter, and she was a warrior. She was held in tremendous esteem by her peers. She was obedient to the Lord, courageous, and stayed true to what God had called her to be.

The Bible tells us in Judges 4:8 that Barak would not go to war unless Deborah went with him and fought. She agreed to go to battle but responded, "However, there will be no glory for you in the course you are taking, for then the Lord will deliver Sisera into the hands of a woman" (Judges 4:9). And that's exactly what happened.

I once heard someone say, 'where you see the oppression of women, you see the antichrist spirit.' Satan has a special enmity for woman and her seed, and he will do anything to oppress her. The oppression of women has done a great disservice to her collective identity and needs to be restored. It has equally done a great disservice to the collective body of Christ. Jesus sees men and women as His triumphant, powerful bride.

We see this truth further evidenced in Proverbs 31, when it references a 'noble woman.' This passage is the only time in the Old Testament in which the Hebrew word *'chayil'* is translated 'noble,' because it describes a woman. Everywhere else we see the word, it is in reference to soldiers, and is closer to the words: 'valiant, army, power, might, warrior.'

Proverbs 31 is actually ripe with military language, as Suzy Silk points out, "The word for 'buying' means 'she hunts out prey and she brings it back. And when it says that 'she puts on clothes', it's actually 'she girds her loins with strength.' There is so much military language in that passage…English translators (who were mostly men) had seen her as the epitome of a quiet, submissive, noble European woman. I realized she was actually the warrior woman Eve was meant to be."[16]

The Passion Translation comes the closest to the original language. Verse 10 says, "Who could ever find a wife like this one- she is a woman of strength and mighty valor!" Verse 17 says, "She wraps herself in strength, might, and power in all her works." Verse 25 says, "Bold power and glorious majesty are wrapped around her as she laughs with joy over the latter days."

I love the footnote in The Passion Translation for Proverbs 31:10, "…The subject is the perfect bride, the virtuous woman. This woman is both a picture of a virtuous wife and **an incredible allegory of the end-time victorious bride of Jesus Christ, full of virtue and grace**."

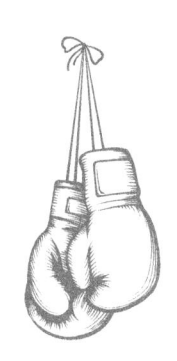

UNION RESERVOIR
Introducing Destiny

My daughter loves to jump in puddles and splash water around like only a toddler can. We recently moved to a new town and happened to live within walking distance to a reservoir. I decided to plan a special day for us to enjoy the swim beach at this reservoir near our new home. I had prepared the stroller, packed all the gear I thought we would need, and got us out the door.

We made it to the sidewalk only for my daughter to become fixated on a puddle, as it had rained the night before. Knowing we were headed to a reservoir, which would be a million times more exciting than splashing in a little two-foot-wide puddle, I began to plead with her to trust me. The resolve of toddlers though can be incredible, which is especially true of my toddler.

Nevertheless, I stood there begging, "Harper, please, just trust mommy. I have something very exciting planned for us. Something way more exciting than this little puddle. Please, come on! Please just trust me!"

Then I felt it. The Lord tapped on my shoulder and I suddenly realized He had been asking me the same thing; "Ya' listening, baby girl? Will you please just trust Me? I have something amazing planned, but we can't go there unless you trust Me."

ZING!

My only response at this point was, "Ok, Lord, where do I begin."

He asked me to read Song of Songs. He also told me He would speak to me our entire journey to the reservoir, as He wanted to show me things to come. As if on cue, my toddler conceded, compliantly climbing into the stroller so we could begin our journey. Toddler's do much more of the Lord's bidding then we realize.

I couldn't remember the last time I had read Song of Songs. As I was processing it with the Lord, I felt like He was showing me it was all about a coming revival- a great end-time harvest. I asked Him if I was discerning this correctly.

He responded, "Where are you headed right now?"

"A Reservoir." I said.

He then asked, "Yes, what's the name of the reservoir?"

"UNION." I responded. And at this, I stopped in my tracks in reverent awe, as the fear of the Lord became tangible to me. As you likely know, 'union,' among other things, is a word used to describe matrimony. The culmination of love.

As I looked up from my shocked stupor, I suddenly realized I was standing on a road between two wheat fields. The field on the right had already been harvested and the field on the left was ripe for harvest. The Lord showed me the field which had already been harvested was the body of Christ, and the field ripe for harvest was our mission field for what is coming. He told me this coming revival was for both fields. Not only to bring souls into the kingdom but also to restore Christians back to passionate first love. Somehow, under all our programs and systems, the Lord has become too familiar for us and we need to renew our passionate wonder in the fire of His love.

As we approached the reservoir, near the entrance was a post with a cross on it. The gate connected to the post was closed. I could sense there were many in the body of Christ who will be closed-off to this next move of God because it will not look the way they are expecting it to. And it will involve people they are not expecting it to. I honestly wasn't exactly sure what that even meant, until we arrived at the reservoir.

As we arrived, I was overwhelmed at the diversity I saw. There were all sort of people there- different types of families, different ethnicities, homosexuals and heterosexuals, all ages, and all sizes. I thought to myself, 'this is it. This is your end-time harvest. It is the most diverse collection of people I have ever seen gathered in one place.'

Many in the church have been enslaved to a religious spirit, and this has hindered His love. But He wants them all. He loves them all. He died for them all. We need to see people who are different from us through the lens of the cross and lose our ability to be offended. His end-time harvest is going to be the most diverse conglomerate of souls and ministers ever seen.

We like things and people we can control because it gives us a false sense of comfort and security. Let me put you on notice now- this coming revival is going to be anything but safe. The sooner we can ditch fear, offenses, and self-righteous judgement- the sooner we can see Heaven invade earth.

We have become so labor oriented with the Lord; we've forgotten how to be loved and extend love. He didn't put us here so we could run around busy until our time is up. We are here to learn how to be loved and how to love. He wants us to know how He feels about us. How He sees us.

Revelation 19 is filled with celebration as all of heaven rejoices that the bride has made herself ready and the wedding of the Lamb has come. The words 'has made herself ready' come from the Greek word '*hetoimasen*.' It is a cognate of the word '*hetoimos*,' which means 'ready because the necessary preparations are done.' We need to be intentional about sitting with the Holy Spirit and letting Him help us get ready.

"The Spirit and the bride say, "Come!" And let the one who hears say, "Come!" Let the one who is thirsty come; and let the one who wishes take the free gift of the water of life" (Revelation 22:17; NIV).

One of the main assignments of the Holy Spirit is to prepare for Jesus a bride. The Spirit and the bride are both able to say "come!" in this passage because they have both done the work of preparing the bride. It is in this reverent awe of His love, that I share what I have in this book.

I hope it rouses the sleeping giant of His bride from her slumber. I hope it liberates her from every oppressive religious spirit and pharisaical bondage. I hope it awakens her to surrender to love. I hope it reveals her authority in Christ. I hope it ignites a fire in her that cannot be suffocated. I hope it births renewal, so renewal can birth reformation. And lastly, I hope she is not offended at how, and whom, the Lord chooses to accomplish this awakening.

"The end-time church must be equipped with the revelation of God's love and beauty to walk in victory in the midst of the most emotionally wounded and sexually broken generation in history."[17] Mike Bickle

We have already talked about the powerful, radiant Bride of Proverbs 31 (The Passion Translation). Proverbs 31 isn't just for women however; it is also a picture of the Bride of Christ- His end-time triumphant bride. The Hebrew word used in this passage to describe the wife is the word '*khayil*.' It is such a dynamic word, it can mean 'powerful, wealthy, righteous, efficient, mighty like an army, military force, strength, valor, excellence, worthy.' This is His army- warriors clothed in love.

After my daughter and I had returned from Union Reservoir, I immediately cracked open Song of Songs, as the Lord had asked me to. I'm going to be honest with you; it was painful! I don't remember what translation I was reading, but I was fighting tooth and nail to finish.

Finally saying to the Lord, "I have no idea what you are trying to show me. This is painful. Animals, body parts, and flames, oh my!"

Introducing Destiny

I set it down in total agony. This was going to be so much harder than I thought. I didn't pick it back up for a couple weeks because I just honestly didn't know where to start. Then it occurred to me that maybe there was another translation which presented it in a way I could understand. Or at least I hoped so.

I started looking for different translations and discovered The Passion Translation. In this translation, I read through the book in what felt like a heartbeat, crying my eyes out the entire time. I could finally grasp 'it' and 'it' was glorious! I highly recommend you do the same. It will impart fire to your heart. If it weren't for the copyright, I would have copied and pasted the entire book right here and said, "it is finished."

The Passion Translation has changed my life. I don't know how else to explain it. You need it in your life. I recently learned Song of Songs was the first book they translated, as it is the translator's favorite book of the Bible. It is a beautiful work of art.

"I have attempted to translate not only from a scholarly or linguistic perspective, but also from the passion of a heart on fire. Love will always find a language to express itself...I believe the Holy Spirit has hidden within the Song of Songs an amazing story- a story of how Jesus makes his bride beautiful and holy by casting out her fear with perfect love." (Introduction, The Passion Translation, 2018, Second Edition, Pg.1020).

Song of Songs, or Song of Solomon depending on your translation, is about the journey of divine romance. The main characters in the book are King Solomon (symbolizing the Bridegroom King, Jesus), the Shulamite (symbolizing us as the corporate Bride of Christ), Daughters/Maidens/Brides-to-Be of Jerusalem (symbolizing sincere but spiritually immature believers), and The Watchmen (symbolizing spiritual leaders).

The bride is referred to as the Shulamite, and the bridegroom is often referred to as Solomon. As The Passion Translation points out, 'Shulamite' and 'Solomon' both come from the same Hebrew root word, one is feminine form and the other masculine form (*'Hassulammit'* and *'Bassulammit'*). From the beginning we understand they are one, as even their names are one. In this book Solomon is meant to point us to Jesus. We are one with Him- the two becoming one, in union with even His name. This is our destiny, our DNA, our covenant promise.

The book has two primary themes. The first four chapters we observe the focus is mainly on the Bride's inheritance in Christ. We learn from them how the Lord sees us and loves us; it is all about who we are in Him. The last four chapters mainly focus on Jesus' inheritance in us, His Bride. They highlight for us what Jesus seeks from us. He wants us to love Him with all that we are, not just the best parts of who we are.

I always thought the cross was the end of the story, but now I know it isn't enough for you just to know His salvation. He wants to know you as well. He wants you to share your life with Him too. This is part of what He paid for; to have a mutual inheritance in one another, an essential for any great relationship.

This always reminds me of His caution in Matthew 7:22-23, "Many will say to Me on that day, 'Lord, Lord, did we not prophesy in Your name, and in Your name cast out demons and in Your name perform many miracles? And then I will declare to them, 'I never knew you; depart from Me, you who practice lawlessness!'"

Yikes! I don't want to be that guy! We had better dive into Song of Songs so we can learn how to let His love all the way in, and how to remain in abiding love.

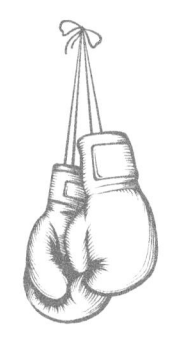

DISCOVERY OF LOVE
Awakening The Heart

I want to share a vision with you that I believe will help illustrate how Jesus sees us and how He loves us. When I arrived at Youth with A Mission (YWAM) for a Discipleship Training School (DTS), in 2007, I had a powerful encounter with Jesus. Our first day in class, my school leader asked each of us to spend a few minutes with the Lord. We were to ask Him if there was anything He wanted to reveal to us, either for our lives or for our time at DTS.

I had a vision and I saw Jesus standing over a patch of dirt. He was wearing a war drum and He stood over this patch of dirt, faithfully playing the drum, obviously waiting for something to happen. I suddenly realized I was the patch of dirt. He was beating the drum, waiting for me to 'come to life.' I arose from the dirt and stood before Him.

He looked at me and said, 'I LOVE YOU."

I told Him that I loved Him too and He said, "NO. YOU DON'T UNDERSTAND WHAT I MEAN."

As He said this, a giant music staff popped up in the sky. I saw a multitude of notes populate the staff. As I stared at it, I realized their shape formed an outline of mountains and valleys.

He said, "IT DOESN'T MATTER WHERE YOU HAVE BEEN IN LIFE, WHETHER YOU WERE ON A MOUNTAIN OR IN A

VALLEY, MY LOVE FOR YOU HAS NEVER CHANGED." Then I saw the words 'GREAT AWAKENING,' and the vision ended.

Historically, drums have been used in war for all manner of reasons, but namely: to summon the war, to synchronize the march of the soldiers, and to communicate commands from officers to soldiers. They are commonly thought of as symbols to the rhythm of life, and often equated to the beating of the human heart.

All of heaven is fighting a battle for your heart. Jesus hung on a cross with your heart in mind. Love is the currency of heaven. Love is why we are here. 'Loved' is how heaven sees you. If you are born again, you have a mandate to fight for love. We are in a war over love.

The heartbeat of Jesus Christ pulses through our veins. The Father that created you, now hunts for your heart. Nothing can separate us from the love of God in Christ Jesus. As I sat their thinking about the vision, I remembered that my name means 'Beloved' in English and 'Melody' in French. With this, we need to dive into Song of Songs, the great love song of Jesus and His triumphant bride.

Song of Songs starts out with the Shulamite petitioning the Bridegroom to draw her into his heart. She is asking him to reveal himself to her, though she is fully aware of how unworthy she is. She begins from the place of surrender. Even though all she can see is her own darkness, all he acknowledges is her light.

"The paradox of our faith is that we are dark in our own heart, yet we are lovely to God. That is the great paradox that a lot of believers never ever settle. We are dark in our own hearts; that is talking about our own fallenness and sinfulness. Because of the grace of God, we are lovely to God, and God actually enjoys His relationship with us even in our weakness. Beloved, this one truth will change your life radically. You land this, you get this established in your heart, and you will run to Him and not from Him when you discover your weakness and failure" [18] (Mike Bickle).

In verse 2, the Shulamite asks him to smother her with kisses. Strong's 5401 identifies, 'Let him kiss me' from the Hebrew word for 'kiss' as '*nashaq*,' which can also mean 'to fasten up, to equip with weapons, armed for battle, rule[19]. The primitive word '*nasaq*' means 'to burn or kindle, or cause to go up in flame as an offer of sacrifice.' This is what His word does for us, it equips us, arms us, prepares us to rule, sets our hearts on fire, purifies our sacrifice, and so much more!

In verse 4 she asks Him again to draw her into his heart, into his cloud filled chamber. This is speaking two things: one- being drawn into his heart and his innermost being (heart chamber) and his fragrant spices within, two- it is pointing us back to the Holy of Holies inside the temple chamber. One day a year, on the Day of Atonement, coals from the altar were combined with two handfuls of incense. This was then taken into the Holy of Holies, where the incense was made to smoke before the mercy seat of the Ark of Covenant (Leviticus 16:12-13).

She is aware of her darkness and sin and she is asking him to 'kiss,' to burn up in flame as an offer of sacrifice, the things that separate them so her darkness can be atoned for and she can enter the innermost chamber, where they can be intimately connected. She wants nothing between them, but she doesn't yet know what it's going to cost her to get to that place of intimacy and fellowship.

She then continues to persist at how dark she is and how sinful her ways have been, and he continues to only call her 'lovely.' In fact, he compares her to the fine linen tapestry hanging in the Holy Place. The knowledge of how God feels about us, sees us, loves us- it has the power to heal our wounds and bind up our brokenness. How we see God is of equal importance.

In verse 7, she clearly sees him as a shepherd when she asks him where he feeds his flock that she might follow. Declaring she wishes to be fully cloaked by him as she wanders amongst his flock. She wants nothing between them. This is evidenced further when she says, "It is you I long for, with no veil between us!" (Song of Songs 1:7 TPT).

As we've discussed in previous chapters, in the temple, the veil (curtain) served as a barrier to the Holy of Holies, where only the high priest could enter. Within the Holy of Holies was the Ark of Covenant, where His presence was manifested. She is essentially asking to never know a day without his presence.

Our greatest fear is that people will see behind our façade, they will see the real us and consequently not love us. This is a lie. Jesus sees her fully and loves her fully. It is beautiful to me that while she is only aware of her darkness, he only sees her light. In verse 8 he addresses her as 'radiant one,' and in verse 11 He speaks of enhancing it, claiming she will be marked with redeeming grace.

She then identifies his crucifixion (symbolized by the myrrh), resting over her heart. She understands he was crucified for love. *'Engedi'* means 'fountain of the Lamb, and the Hebrew word for *'henna'* is 'hakkoper,' and means 'ransom.' With this we transition from the Old Testament model of Ark of the Covenant, to the crucifixion of Jesus Christ. The revelation of His love, as the suffering lover of the cross, overwhelms her heart as she declares she will hold him and never let him part. She tells us their resting place is anointed and flourishing and, "The beams of our house are cedars; our rafters, cypresses" (Song of Songs 1:17).

Cypress is an evergreen tree. As we discussed in a previous chapter, evergreen trees are a symbol of eternal covenant. Symbolically, to have something over your head, is a symbol of being under its covering. For the rafters to be made of cypress, we can understand from this verse that their love is under the covering of eternal covenant. It is secure. Their love is dwelling in eternal promise.

Cedar was commonly burned in cleansing ceremonies for purification. So, when she tells us their beams are cedar and their rafters are cypresses; she is saying their resting place is built on (made stable because of) the purification she now has through suffering love (the cross), which is covered (rafters) by the eternal covenant of God. She is boxed-in by love. Completely surrounded by it.

Isaiah 55:13 declares, "Instead of the thorn bush the cypress will come up, and instead of the nettle the myrtle will come up, and it will be a memorial to the Lord, for an everlasting sign which will not be cut off."

The thorn bush is a symbol for the curse of sin (Genesis 3:18). Jesus wore a crown of thorns on the cross, taking away the curse of sin. Which allows us to enter into eternal covenant with God. Doubt is replaced with God's promised blessings springing up. The crucifixion is a memorial to our Lord, an everlasting sign and eternal covenant that cannot be undone.

The Shulamite is now fully aware of these truths and awakened to the love that empowers them. In Chapter 2 we come to understand that he is free and leaping over the mountains that separate them, but she is surrounded by fear and religious duty. She hears him coming to her, bounding with joy over the things that separate them.

"...Now he comes closer, **even to the places where I hide**. He gazes into my soul, peering through the portal as he blossoms within my heart" (Song of Songs 2:9; TPT).

This is beautiful. She is telling us that not only is he growing within her, but he watches over that growth from outside. We understand from this verse she has not yet surrendered everything to him. He peers into her soul, as he observes his love beginning to blossom within her, but he is not inhabiting it yet. She hasn't let him all the way in yet. Are there rooms in your heart which are off-limits to the Lord?

Upon this, he beckons to her to arise, for he longs to draw her to his heart. He declares her barren winter is over and the season of hiding is gone. It is time for pruning.

"Can you not discern this new day of destiny breaking forth around you? The early signs of my purposes and plans are bursting forth" (Song of Songs 2:13; TPT).

He petitions her to catch the foxes (v. 2:15); the compromises of sin, the hidden hurts we keep in our hearts. These are areas in our life we have not yet surrendered to Christ. They stand as monuments- inhibiting love and limiting our ability to receive His love. They infiltrate our identity, habits, and desires. They hijack our future. It is time to prune these places in her heart as He wants all of her.

Lilies are symbols of purity. Verse 2:16 says, 'He browses among the lilies." The word used here for browse is *'ra'ah.'* It is the same word used in Psalm 23 for, "The Lord is my Shepherd." We can understand from this that He is shepherding her heart and leading it to purity. She can only see darkness, but His shepherd rod and staff are leading her through the valley of shadows and into transformative light.

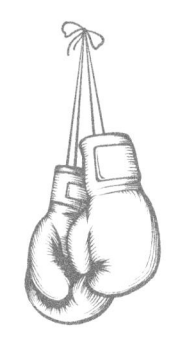

CATCHING FOXES
Slaying The Giants Within

In chapter two, he beckoned her to run away with him, but she is so overcome by the shadows of fear, she tells him to go on without her and she will come away another time. Fear is the opposite of love, and love is the antidote to fear. The Shulamite was overwhelmed by shifting shadows of fear. She could see his love, but she could not feel his love. At this, we need to address some common 'foxes' that will keep you held back.

Fear

Fear is one of the most prevalent assignments the enemy unleashes to keep us constrained to our past and hindered from walking in all that Jesus died for. I have a very interesting testimony I would like to share with you about something amazing the Lord revealed to me regarding fear.

It started for me when I was working as an accounting clerk and still finishing up my college internship. To juggle both, I sustained a bizarre work schedule for a semester. One morning I drove into the parking lot at 4am for my accounting job and there were police cars in the parking lot, but I did not see police anywhere. The building was dark as the main lights did not turn on until 6am.

Through dimly lit safety lights however, I could see a flashlight flickering through the window, at the other end of the building.

Still not sure what was going on, I entered the building and headed straight for the flashlights, which led me to a deck on the backside of the building. I found two police officers on the deck who informed me they had responded to a building alarm which went off. It was very windy that morning, and after having walked the perimeter of the building, they told me they suspected the wind must have caught one of the deck doors and triggered the building alarm.

With this, they left, and as soon as they did, I realized they told me they had only walked the perimeter of the building and didn't bother to check either floor of the interior of the building for intruders. A bit frightened, I tried to keep my cool. I took the word 'accounting' literal, as I sat in my dark cubicle 'ah-counting' minutes, hoping for a coworker to arrive sooner than normal.

At the peak of my unproductivity, I heard a loud bang from the floor below me. It sounded like a shot gun went off. Panicked, I ran to an empty office, locked the door even though all the doors were made of glass, hid under the desk and called 911 to report a break-in and gunshots.

As I was on the phone with 911, I saw a man I had never met before walk right past the office I was hiding in. Honestly, I held my breath as I thought I was about to die. Still on the phone with 911 and unsure where the man was at this point, a coworker showed up for work early, saying my name as she got closer to my cubicle. Terrified she was about to be shot and/or expose my hiding place, I opened the door and yanked her into the office, quickly briefing her about what was going on. And then we both crawled under the desk to hide some more.

It was at this point the police officers showed back up, looking through the building windows and doors. I saw the intruder re-appear, walking towards them. Panicking for their safety, I began frantically trying to tell the 911 operator the suspect was approaching the police officers and they needed to take some cover. It didn't get conveyed in time and the man opened the door the officers were standing at. I could see him talking with the officers, but I wasn't sure what about. I kept stressing to the operator the police were now talking to the suspect, and she needed to warn them.

This next part is a bit embarrassing. As it turns out, the man was covering for the normal property manager who was on vacation, which explains why I didn't recognize him. He too was responding to the same building alarm the cops had initially responded to and the very loud bang, was in fact, the wind ripping the deck door open. All one very big misunderstanding, which I never lived down. My coworkers taped a sign to the office I hid in that read, "Carrie's Panic Room."

The entire experience, though none of it ending up as a real physical threat, had done a great deal to affect me. I found myself in incredible fear, constantly. Suddenly I couldn't sleep in the dark but had to leave lights on. Always looking over my shoulder, everywhere I went. Even the silence bothered me, and I had to have constant worship playing just to calm my nerves. I was suffering serious post-traumatic stress to an onset of fear that had hijacked my life. It crippled me for months. As an adult, I was too embarrassed to tell anyone. I just kept it a secret and tried to cope and adapt to my new normal.

While this had been going on for several months, the Lord had simultaneously called me out of the accounting job, and I was now teaching full time at the Christian school I had interned for. The pay was not substantial and many of the teachers, including myself, scraped to make ends meet. After I paid my bills every month, I had $50 left to get me through the month for groceries and gas. I tell people I lived on rice and beans, but it was honestly mostly rice.

One day I received a gift from my parents- a case of good organic chicken sausage. It would have set me up nicely for a while and I was certainly hungry for it. As I was thinking about all the different seasonings I could add to chicken sausage, rice, and beans to pretend I was eating various meals- I felt the Holy Spirit nudging me to share my bounty. Honestly, I struggled with the decision all day and all night. Keep in mind, all of this was going on while I was still gripped in fear.

The next morning, standing at my kitchen sink before work, I resolved to obey the Holy Spirit and ignore my hunger. As soon as I made my resolve to share the meat with my coworkers, I had a vision. If you ever find yourself in a hard place needing breakthrough, start looking for things to give away. Generosity is a magnet for breakthrough. And there is a difference between giving from a place of abundance and giving from a place of need. The Lord sees both, but they tap into different resources from Heaven.

In the vision, I could see myself from Heaven's perspective. I was standing at my kitchen sink and I could see the demon that had been crouched over me, tormenting me in fear. I immediately pointed to it, exclaiming to the Lord, "That's it! That thing has been tormenting me for months!"

The Lord responded, "YES, I KNOW. LOOK CLOSER."

As I looked closer, I could see the demon curled up in fear itself. It was carrying out its assignment of fear against me, but it clearly looked more terrified then even I was at this point- after months of torment. I stood there for a moment, wide-eyed, as I watched it trembling.

Confused, I asked, "Lord, I don't understand? This thing has been tormenting me for months. Why does it look more afraid then I am? Why is it looking at me terrified?"

He responded, "BECAUSE IT KNOWS AT ANY MOMENT, YOU COULD HAVE A REVELATION OF THE AUTHORITY YOU HAVE OVER IT."

Selah.

The vision ended. Still standing at my kitchen sink, but now armed with revelation- I felt anticipation starting to supplant fear. I Immediately confessed my sin for believing fears' lies, broke agreement with those lies, and took authority over it in Jesus Name- commanding it to leave. That was the end of a long season of fear. It was finished.

Did you know the enemy lives in fear over the revelation of your destiny being made known to you? You do now!

HOPE DEFERRED

There is another root of fear we need to address; one that results from hope deferred. When you walk through a false start, or death of a vision, hope deferred can take root. It sews lies into your very core, causing you to question if you can even hear the voice of God correctly. The despair that visits us on the heels of hope deferred can become a beautiful opportunity of refining if we will allow it. Purifying our heart and refining our motives, it asks the question, "will you seek Me for Me, and not just for the rewards that come with seeking Me?"

"When hope's dream seems to drag on and on, the delay can be depressing. But when at last your dream comes true, life's sweetness will satisfy your soul" (Proverbs 13:12; TPT).

One thing we need to watch out for after a season of hope deferred is the fear of hoping again. We can become 'gun-shy' in trusting the Lord's goodness again. I urge you, trust the Lord, no matter what your emotions or the spirit of fear are screaming at you. Like Sarah, count Him faithful, despite all odds. He truly can do immeasurably more than we could ever imagine. Don't grow despaired because He chooses to accomplish things in a way you do not understand.

Let the banner over your heart read, 'thus saith the Lord,' instead of 'thus saith me.' Needing to be in control is a force of manipulation, set-up as a false sense of comfort. It convinces you that being in control will bubble-wrap you from life's troubles and disappointments. This is not biblical, and it is also not Jesus' best for us.

When we can reach a place of trust in the Lord where we are no longer engrossed on the desired outcome but simply focused on Him, then we have wholly surrendered our 'yes' to Jesus. When the outcome of my circumstances, nor the circumstances themselves, do not govern whether or not I win, but my simple trust in Him does, then I have surrendered my all to Him. When you know the battle belongs to the Lord, you aren't fixated on the desired outcome or negative circumstances. You are not led astray by your own anticipations.

Battles are never about circumstances. Battles are about trust, and trust is built on covenant. Because I am crucified with Christ, and the Bible clearly teaches us the battle belongs to the Lord- the moment I choose to trust, I have victory. Even before the battle is over, from this posture, I already know I've won. I have a covenantal promise with God that declares my triumph. So, my only 'RESONSE-ibility' is in choosing to trust Him and His covenant promises. The rest is literally and tangibly His.

Psalm 46:10 commands us to, "be still and that I am God." The word 'still' comes from the word '*harpu*,' and means- to relax, to abandon, to withdraw. In other words, 'be still, abandoning your cares, worries, anxieties, and troubles and know that I am God. Give it to Me and be at peace.'

SHAME

I highly encourage you to watch the TED talk by Brene Brown titled, "Listening to Shame." Dr. Brown defines shame as: "Shame is the intensely painful feeling or experience of believing we are flawed and therefore unworthy of love and belonging." She further says, "Owning our story can be hard but not nearly as difficult as spending our lives running from it. Only when we are brave enough to explore the darkness will we discover the infinite power of our light." [20]

Shame can come from a lot of different sources- from the enemy, from family, from ourselves over past mistakes, and even from within the body of Christ. Shame coming from within the body of Christ is the saddest for me to observe, because this is the place people should feel the freest and most accepted. I think it often goes unchecked however, because it doesn't always look like obvious shame, but masquerades itself as 'discernment,' or worse- "speaking the truth in love."

The form of shame I am talking about here, is one that comes from a pharisaical spirit, birthed in unrighteous judgment. It is not from the heart of the Father, though it claims to be. It is the judgment believers cast on others, though they've never walked a minute in that person's shoes or endured the testing fire the Lord has ordained for them. It is a form of persecution that says, "Why do you walk with a limp? Why are doing it that way? See how I am doing it? Try and do it just like me. See how good I am?"

A pharisaical spirit will spotlight flaws, heaping shame on the Father's sons and daughters, multiplying their condemnation. This throws a mantle of shame on people, binding them to our limited oppressive judgment of them. All of this assumes we know more about them and are better able to 'minster' to them, than the Holy Spirits' ability to comfort and lead them. Again, all of this without ever walking a minute in someone's shoes, or on their path, or through their fire of refining and testing.

Be careful to never find yourself walking in this- walking against Jesus. Jesus chooses the weak things of this world to confound the wise. Remember, He came to bind the brokenhearted, to set captives free. Isaiah 54:4-5 says, "Do not fear, for your shame is no more. Do not be embarrassed, for you will not be disgraced.

You will forget the inadequacy you felt in your youth and will no longer remember the shame of your widowhood. For your Maker is your husband; his name is Yahweh, Commander of Angel Armies! Your Kinsman-Redeemer is the Holy One of Israel! He has the title Mighty God of all the Earth" (TPT).

Shame is a demonic force which will attempt to keep you feeling worthless, embarrassed, humiliated, and ultimately- isolated. Shame spins lies to keep you held in its grip, convincing you that if people really knew who you were or the things you have done, then no one would want you or love you. It tells you that if you could just emulate so and so, then you would have value. Its primary goal is to keep you trapped in a net of pain, isolated and powerless.

This couldn't be further from the heart of the Father. Isaiah 61:7 promises, "Instead of your shame you will have a double portion, and instead of humiliation they will shout for joy over their portion. Therefore, they will possess a double portion in their land, Everlasting joy will be theirs."

We can see this evidenced further in Hebrews 12:1-2, "Therefore, since we have so great a cloud of witnesses surrounding us, let us also lay aside every encumbrance and the sin which so easily entangles us, and let us run with endurance the race that is set before us, fixing our eyes on Jesus, the author and perfecter of faith, who for the joy set before Him endured the cross, despising the shame, and has sat down at the right hand of the throne of God."

Jesus despised shame. The original language explains 'despised' as 'seeing as insignificant or detestable, devalued, and not worth paying attention to.' We read from the verse above that His eyes were so fixed on the joy that would come from the cross, He literally gave the shame of hanging on the cross, no thought. It had no place in Him.

We think we will be worthy when _____ (fill in the blank). He says we are worthy now, because it's not about our worthiness, it's about His love. And His love is all about us. We are the source of His affection. We are the destination of His love.

"For the Lord God helps Me, Therefore, I am not disgraced; Therefore, I have set my face like flint, and I know that I will not be ashamed" (Isaiah 50:7).

Where your face goes, the body follows. We set our faces like flint when we settle our resolve to be disciplined and unmoved in our convictions, taking Him at His word. If someone is trying to heap shame on you, despise it as Jesus did. Devalue it, not the person. It has no place in you, and certainly is not from the heart of the Father. If, after reading this, you realize you have been heaping shame on His sons and daughters, REPENT. Do all you can to help restore that person and undo the reproach you have planted and watered.

"Gaze upon Him, join your life with His, and joy will come. Your faces will glisten with glory. You'll never wear that shame-face again" (Psalm 34:5; TPT).

WORRY

Worry is another tactic of the enemy to keep you occupied, hindered, and distracted. Have you ever heard the phrase, 'worry gives a small thing a big shadow?' Sometimes we even use worry as a form of self-preservation called- 'foreboding joy.'

"...I'd argue that joy is probably the most difficult emotion to really feel...In a culture of deep scarcity-of never feeling safe, certain, and sure enough- joy can feel like a setup...we're always waiting for the other shoe to drop" (Brene Brown).

The gospel of Luke tells us Jesus commanded us not to worry, to not let anxiety enter our hearts. It adds nothing to your life, and only takes life from you (Luke 12). This is not a suggestion. It is a command. When we choose to worry, we are telling God we don't trust Him. We don't think He is big enough to meet all of our needs or to care for us well.

"I repeat it: don't let worry enter your life. Live above the anxious cares about your personal needs. People everywhere seem to worry about making a living, but your heavenly Father knows your every need and will take care of you. Each and every day he will supply your needs as you seek his kingdom passionately, above all else. So don't ever be afraid, dearest friends! Your loving Father joyously gives you his kingdom realm with all its promises! So, now, go and sell what you have and give to those in need, making deposits in your account in heaven, an account that will never be taken from you. Your gifts will become a secure and unfailing treasure, deposited in heaven forever" (Luke 12:29-33; TPT).

We see this echoed all throughout the Bible. Psalm 55:22 instructs us to "cast our cares on the Lord." The word for 'cast' in this passage is the word '*shalak*.' It means 'to throw, fling, cast.' David flung a stone at Goliath. You can fling your worry on the Lord. Jesus paid for it at Calvary. You don't own it anymore; it now belongs to Him. David wrote this psalm on the heels of being betrayed. With this in mind, it points us back to our great shepherd. The One who promises to never leave us or forsake us. The One who leads us beside still waters. The One who makes a way where there is none. The One who radiates lights in the midst of our darkness.

Orphan Mindset

Ephesians 1:5 tells us, "He predestined us to adoption as sons through Jesus Christ to Himself, according to the kind intention of His will."

We need to know we were accepted in the beloved before we were ever able to be rejected, even in the womb. Every person is important and holds a special place in God's heart, reserved just for them. Satan's biggest goal on earth is to wreck violence on God's love. To wreck violence on the children of God being able to receive God's love.

Satan is now an orphan- the only one in all of creation who is meant to be; he wants you to share in his fate. When he asks, "Did God really say?" (Sound familiar?) What he was really asking Eve is, "Are you sure God has your best in mind? Are you sure God really loves you?"

This is why the enemy fuels lust. Lust says, 'what you have isn't good enough. Desire something else because that's what you really deserve.' Lust is opposed to love. Lust is a lie. Every deception of the enemy aims at the sole purpose of keeping you from love. Every lie of the enemy has the sole purpose of attacking love. Every dark thing you can imagine in this world has its roots in a lack of love. Therefore, love is the antidote to every struggle you face. Sin separates. Love gathers.

I once heard Kris Vallotton share, "This is the most fatherless generation in American history in which our fathers didn't die in war!"[21]

I would add, with the onslaught of abortion, we are also the most motherless generation in American history. Entire generations of offspring are literally dying off, slaughtered in the womb, because of a lack of love. Satan knows that 'LOVED' is who you really are. He knows it's your destiny. He knows it's your future. When you love yourself, you can love God. When you love yourself and God, you can love your neighbor. When you love yourself, God, and your neighbor- then you can love your enemy.

The antidote to every struggle is to simply learn to live loved. We need to begin every battle by declaring we are loved, and we belong. We fight from that place, hedged into His heart. This was the only action the Shulamite took regarding her darkness. She let His love in, and it transformed her, until at last Jesus called her the 'dayspring.'

IDENTITY – A CRISIS OF ORIGIN AND PURPOSE

I want to begin this section by sharing a quote with you from Kris Vallotton. He says; "I believe the cry for identity is at the root of so much pain and dysfunction. What I see when I look in the mirror, when no one else is defining me for me, is crucial to me."

Satan will do everything he can to keep you from realizing you are loved just as you are. He knows there is nothing that can stop the force of someone wearing the garment of love. Nothing. The cross wasn't just about repayment for our sins. It was about restoring our identity as 'loved.' He made creation and called it 'good.' 'Good' in this passage is derived from a Hebrew word that means 'beautiful.' He looks at what He's made and declares it's beautiful, excellent wonderful, full of His approval and delight. This is how He sees you.

Satan will attack your worth by causing you to question your image- 'Am I too fat? Too thin? Too tall? Too short?' And on and on and on. We believe the lie that if we could just _____ (fill in the blank), then we will really be beautiful, loved, and accepted. Satan attacks our very image because he knows that if he can get you to question your worth, then he can get you to question whether or not you are actually loved.

He tries to get us to follow him down the path of a lie, convincing us we will eventually 'arrive' at a destination of being loved; all the while hoping we won't realize that's what we already are. Loved. Satan did this very thing to Jesus in the desert. Tempting Him with things that already belonged to Him. You are already fiercely loved, fully, just as you are.

Sometimes we find ourselves enslaved because of the actions of others, like Joseph. God always works things together for our good though. The very assaults of the enemy point to the very place we are meant to rule, reign and be free.

I have seen this in my own life. I was molested by a female family member when I was very young. For the sake of conversation, we will call her Bonnie. I did not share this abuse with anyone until I got older. Sexual abuse is a bizarre thing to endure. It leaves the abused cowered in shame, somehow feeling the entire assault was their fault. It is not. But the truth is hard to navigate as a defenseless child.

You cannot endure a trauma like that and come out unscathed-unaffected by the fruit that results from it. Consequently, I learned as a young adult that a couple family members wondered if, as a child, I had a homosexual tendency because of some of the manifestations they observed from my behavior when I was little. I do not.

I was unaware of their suspicion until I became a young adult. Can you imagine how much harder and chaotic my life would have been though if I had known as a child? If it had become my label and the banner over my life? My parents wisely did not share this information with me, and I am so grateful. They did not let it define me. They purposed to love me regardless of whatever I grew up to be. It leads me to wonder though, how many of God's children are enslaved to a lifestyle that has its roots in sexual abuse, trauma, or the opinions, labels, and perverse sway of people in their life?

Can you imagine if I had grown up with parents who unwisely played into this, especially in our WOKE culture today? A culture that teaches children in public schools, starting in kindergarten, about homosexuality and transgenderism.[22] A culture that teaches children not to call their mom and dad, 'mom and dad,' because those labels refer to gender pronouns.[23] A culture that is eliminating gender specific restrooms and locker rooms in schools, which was approved by the Department of Education, under the Obama administration.[24] A culture that teaches twelve-year old's about anal sex, bondage, role playing, blood play, and sex toys.[25] A culture that is introducing abortion clinics in schools and making it possible for kids to get an abortion without parental consent.[26] Children can't smoke, drink, vote, drive, gamble, or obtain credit- but they can kill a baby and chop up their body parts to change their gender. How on earth did we get here?

The 60's in America are known commonly as a time of sexual revolution and so much of the secular world sees this as a positive thing. I wonder how many of those people know the dark 'science' that birthed this revolution?

Alfred Kinsey is considered the father of the sexual revolution. He was an American biologist, professor of entomology and zoology, and a sexologist. He is a Harvard graduate and founded the Institute for Sex Research at Indiana University. He was also a pervert, a sexual criminal, and a pedophile.

His 'science' catapulted the sexual revolution and upheaved our cultural values that drenched the 60's, 70's, 80's, and beyond. His research, and the two books he authored from it, claim that human beings are amoral, and sex driven from birth. It changed the entire way our culture viewed sex.

However, the subjects from which he drew his data were largely from incarcerated sex criminals, prostitutes, his staff (whom he encouraged to have orgies in his attack while he filmed them), and from pedophiles. One of his lesser known data points come from his research titled, The Children of Table 34.[27] This graph is available on the internet. It is a horrific account of children ranging from 5 months old to 14 years old, being molested by an assumed family member. The family member would then report their findings to Alfred Kinsey. Every time the child passed out from the trauma; it was counted as an orgasm. His 'findings' are horrifying: an 11-month-old being molested 10 times in one hour, a 4-year-old being molested 26 times in 24 hours, an 11-year-old being raped 19 times in 1 hour, the list goes on.

Kinsey solicited and encouraged pedophiles to sexually violate 2,035 infants and children, based on known public data, for his 'scientific research,' which he then labeled as 'normal child sexuality.' Sex educators and advocates still quote these child data points as being law; declaring they show children have a need for homosexual, heterosexual, and bisexual satisfaction via 'safe sex' education. To this day, the Kinsey Institute and Indiana University pride themselves on being, and I quote, "the trusted source for scientific knowledge and research on critical issues in sexuality, gender, and reproduction."

All of Kinsey's 'data' is locked away at Indiana University, and I believe this University owes the victims recompense. They have an obligation, in my opinion, to do their best to right this wrong.

"The man heralded with enthusiasm by mainstream publications such as *Time* and *Life Magazine* was nothing less than a monstrous facilitator of child-rape. In fact, he even went so far as to record children shrieking and thrashing in pain, passing out and convulsing as the result of the hellish abuse he was putting them through, as evidence of "orgasm"—especially for children who could not yet speak... Today's pornified sex educators, legal experts, academics, and more disturbingly, pedophile groups such as NAMBLA pushing "inter-generational intimacy," all use Kinsey's work to justify their agendas and lend their causes scientific credibility" (Jonathon Van Maren).

Of Kinsey's research, Dr. Reisman points out:

1. "[Dr. Kinsey's team] 'forced' subjects to give the desired answers to their sex questions,
2. Secretly trashed three quarters of their research data, and
3. Based their claims about normal males on a roughly 86 percent aberrant male population including 200 sexual psychopaths, 1,400 sex offenders and hundreds each of prisoners, male prostitutes and promiscuous homosexuals. Moreover, so few normal women would talk to them that the Kinsey team labeled women who lived over a year with a man

'married,' reclassifying data on prostitutes and other unconventional women as "Susie Homemaker."

Without the Rockefeller Foundation, Kinsey could not have become the household name that birthed the sexual revolution. Without Kinsey's launching of the sexual revolution and Hefner's success as Kinsey's pamphleteer, Planned Parenthood would not be the multi-billion-dollar abortion and birth control giant now benefiting from Rockefeller's successors. In 1915, the year that David Rockefeller was born, Supreme Court Justice Louis Brandeis testified about the dangers that could arise from powerful philanthropic influence masked as benevolence. Rockefeller Foundation's sponsorship of Kinesy's child rape-based sexual freedom agenda and its domino effect on law, society and culture, our modern child porno-criminal, pedophile and trafficking epidemics, and the eugenics-based work of Planned Parenthood, which justifies killing millions of unborn children, has certainly proven the truth of Justice Brandeis predictions."[28]

We can learn a lot from history. James Shupe, a retired United States Army soldier, is a man who once experienced gender identity crisis. He was the first person in the United States to become labeled 'nonbinary,' through an elaborate court case. His case is still used in court today to validate this agenda. What no one talks about however, is he experienced massive regret over his transition and eventually went to great efforts to reverse it back, as he was originally designed. A judge approved the court order to reverse his decision, and James is now a vocal critic of gender identity transition.

What he shares about his experience is enlightening for us all, "The mental health system just rubber stamps you with gender dysphoria and they don't look at the underlying behavior. Educating myself about why I was doing the things I was doing was key to being able to make peace with it and allow me to get back to reality."²⁹

Until recently, transgenderism was considered a mental health disorder in the Diagnostic and Statistical Manual of Mental Disorders (DSM-V). Now it is used simply to diagnose distress caused by the perception of gender mismatch.

Let me illustrate the power of influence those in our lives have to impact who we become. The same family member that used to molest me, Bonnie, would often lock me up in a crawl space in her house periodically, when my sister and I would spend the weekend with her. I would usually never see it coming, but she would grab me and put me in this room. Time is a hard thing for children to grasp, but it felt like she would leave me in there for hours. This small room became a dark cave for me, where I would sit shrouded in rejection, wondering why I was so hard to love. Wondering what was wrong with me. I didn't tell my parents about this until I became an adult because I thought I was the problem.

This had an incredible impact on me. I grew up with an overwhelming sense of being unlovable despite my parent's affection for me. I felt invisible, and unwanted. I just assumed people would reject me. I can remember as early as middle school, spending every lunch hour hiding in a bathroom stall so I wouldn't have to enter the lunchroom and face assumed rejection from my peers. I would sit in the stall and wait to hear the bell ring so I could go to my next class. I was a very lonely kid, but I told no one.

I will never forget, years later, being at an event and a stranger approached me out of nowhere and said, 'you grew up thinking no one loved you, but you are one of His favorites.' As you can imagine, I cried, hard. My name means 'beloved,' but I had a hard time believing anyone did. As I said in the beginning of this section, the enemy will attack the very thing you are destined to be.

Satan always tries to counterfeit the things of God. In fact, I believe this WOKE culture is, in some way, a prophetic declaration for us. God's prophets have been declaring a Third Great Awakening is coming to America for a while now. WOKE is a word play on the word AWAKE. WOKE is all about being mindful of social injustices and the 'underdogs' of society. However, it's being used by the enemy to push an agenda of perversion. If ever there was a person in all human history who embraced underdogs and fought against injustice, it was Jesus Christ. The coming Third Great Awakening is going to reform our entire nation and return us back to first love and His original design for us.

The enemy is prophesying our future, like the enemy did to Gideon. In Judges 7 the Lord instructed Gideon to sneak down into the enemies' camp to hear what they were saying about Gideon. The Lord tells Gideon that what he overhears from the mouth of the enemy will strengthen him. This is what Gideon hears the enemy saying about him, "This is nothing less than the sword of Gideon the son of Joash, a man of Israel; God has given Midian and all the camp into his hand" (Judges 7:14).

Gideon and his 300 mighty men go on to defeat the Midianites, an army without number.

We will experience a Third Great Awakening in America; I think it is even starting to begin now. Until it arrives fully, will we choose to focus on the report of the ten spies Joshua sent out, or focus on the abundance the Lord is bringing in, like Caleb? The enemy is indeed sowing confusion in sexuality and gender. Compassion and mercy will be the forerunners to anyone desiring to minister here.

Jeffrey McCall is a man who has supernaturally found freedom from the transgender and male prostitute lifestyle, through the miraculous grace of God. He now leads a ministry to help others who are bound but want to be free. You can learn more about this amazing ministry by visiting freedommarch.com.

To quote Lou Engle, "I hope it brings healing and hope for those yearning for freedom…It's time for God to reveal a love for this generation that is stronger than death itself. A flame that is stronger than the flames of a lust-filled culture."

"Stop imitating the ideals and opinions of the culture around you but be inwardly transformed by the Holy Spirit through a total reformation of how you think. This will empower you to discern God's will as you live a beautiful life, satisfying and perfect in His eyes" (Romans 12:2; TPT).

UNFORGIVENESS

A common saying about unforgiveness goes something like this, "unforgiveness tends to hurt the one withholding forgiveness more than the one in need of forgiveness." Finding our way to forgiveness though can be a messy process. When we don't forgive, we become hardened, untrusting, bitter, and in some cases vengeful. It will eat you alive, open you up to demonic attack, and keep you living in the past.

Jesus preached about forgiving as many times as is necessary. Jesus wants you free from hurt and offense. He wants you to forgive others as freely as He has forgiven you. This often trips us up. When we've committed an offense, we plead for grace. When someone has offended us, we plead for justice to be served.

Choosing to forgive is an opportunity from the Lord to fellowship with the cross. It absolutely costs us something. It's meant to. The cross cost Jesus His life. If we truly want to be Christlike, it will cost us the same. Forgiving means we don't get to bring the matter up anymore. Forgiving means we must let go of the ways we have allowed the offense to define us. Forgiving means we must choose love. And sometimes, forgiving takes lots and lots of attempts until you are finally free.

This past Christmas was a hard one for me. I was dealing with some new personal hurt over a matter that involved Bonnie, whom I've shared about in previous sections of this chapter. My family and I were at Christmas worship service together, and towards the end of the service, my pastor encouraged us all to reach out to a family member we don't normally talk to and tell them we love them and merry Christmas.

The Lord immediately spoke to me and said, "I want you to call Bonnie."

I swallowed hard. I had two choices; stay locked in offense or obey the Lord. I chose to obey and told the Lord I would do it tomorrow. Perhaps hoping a little bit that He might forget He had asked me to do it.

The next day, on my way to the grocery store, the Lord said, "I asked you to call Bonnie."

He's really good at remembering stuff. I parked the car, took a few very deep breaths, said a quick prayer, and called Bonnie. I need to admit I was abundantly relieved when she didn't pick up the phone, but now I had all of five seconds to decide if I was going to leave a voicemail or not. I was arguing with myself; "He said call, He didn't say leave a message. Shoot! I don't know what to do! I don't know if I can do this! This hurts! I don't like this!"

I left Bonnie a message. I told Bonnie I was thinking about her and I loved her, and I hoped she had a Merry Christmas. Then I hung up the phone and cried. I didn't understand why, or even how, the Lord could ask me to do that. Leading up to this moment however, I had previously been studying the crucifixion. And, as plain as day, I heard the Lord say, "I am inviting you to fellowship with my crucifixion."

If you can't find it within yourself to forgive someone for your own sake, look a little deeper within yourself, and see if you can do it for the Lord's sake.

"For to me, to live is Christ and to die is gain" (Philippians 1:21).

IN CLOSING

Some of us have lived with 'foxes' for so long, it has become comfortable. Like reaching for your favorite pair of sweatpants, day after day, clothing yourself in the false comfort it provides. It has become so familiar to us, when favor and abundance knock on our door, we don't know how to welcome them in. You can unknowingly become so comfortable with cloaks of darkness that you miss your opportunities for inheritance and upgrade. I would strongly urge you to spend some time with Holy Spirit and ask Him if there is anything in your life He has been trying to get your attention about.

Conversely, we need to be careful we don't do the opposite; become so habitual about catching foxes, we negate the responsibility of learning to be loved and kissed by grace.

I remember a dream Graham Cooke shared several years ago in which he saw Jesus stomping towards him in a dream.

In the dream, Jesus was shouting, "GIVE ME BACK MY STUFF!!!"

Graham said he was frozen in his tracks in the dream, unsure what the Lord meant.

Jesus demanded, "ANXIETY, FEAR, WORRY…I PAID A PRICE FOR IT, GIVE ME BACK MY STUFF! I DIED FOR IT; YOU CAN'T HAVE IT ANYMORE!"

Then Jesus' posture softened as he shared, "I was thrilled to hang on a cross, to take all that stuff from you. I was delighted to do it because I saw you free. And here you are, living in all that stuff I died to take away from you. If you keep all that stuff, I can't give you all the stuff I want to give you. If you keep all that fear, you'll never learn perfect love."

Selah.

Because He loves me, I choose to be fully transformed. I choose to invite His love into every cave of my heart, until His blood has thoroughly pumped through me and given me power to fly. I choose to be transformed so that I can love as He does. I choose to love His children because He says they are worthy, because He says they are loved. The stone in my sling is 'LOVE.'

"Of all powers, love is the most powerful and the most powerless. It is the most powerful because it alone can conquer that final and most impregnable stronghold which is the human heart. It is the most powerless because it can do nothing except by consent" (Frederick Buechner).

In closing, Corinthians 13:13 says, "Three things will last forever- faith, hope, and love- and the greatest of these is love."

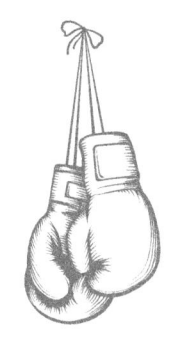

BECAUSE HE SAYS SO
The Transforming Power Of His Love

'Catching Foxes' was a long chapter, but we needed to understand why it's important to confront those things that hide in us and keep us from love. Now that we've done that, let's get back to Song of Songs.

Chapter 3 opens with the Shulamite travailing over her decision to not go to the holy mountains of separation with him. She is enduring a dark night of the soul; a place of spiritual desolation where nothing will bring relief but finding him again.

She chose not to obey his request to come away, and it's almost as if she is being disciplined for it, through an inability to discern or find his presence. The Lord promises to never leave us or forsake us, but sometimes we lose the ability to discern His presence for a season.

The void is more than she can handle, and eventually becomes the catalyst for obedience. She leaves her former place of content, searching everywhere for Him until at last she finds Him. She is so grateful, she fastens herself to him, declaring she will now bring Him within her temple, into her innermost parts. Her heart.

"God wants to purify our minds until we can bear all things, believe all things, hope all things, and endure all things. God dwells in you, but you cannot have this divine power until you live and walk in the Holy Ghost, until the power of the new life is greater than the old life" (Smith Wigglesworth).

It is on the heels of her fastening that the voice of the Lord arrives on the scene, proclaiming the entrance of the Bridegroom's marriage carriage. It's surrounded by angelic warriors, the mightiest of Israel's hosts, standing ready to defend the couple from every terror of night. Remember, 'Israel' means 'God prevails?'

We read of the spices of myrrh and frankincense pillowing the atmosphere as the bridegroom arises from the wilderness. 'Myrrh' is a reference to the suffering love of Christ on the cross, while the 'frankincense' points to His perfect, spotless life.

"The king made this mercy seat for himself...the place where they sit together is sprinkled with crimson. Love and mercy cover this carriage, blanketing his tabernacle throne. The king himself has made it for those who will become his bride" (Song of Songs 3:9-10; TPT).

This passage takes us back to the Ark of the Covenant and points us to our new model for covenant: Jesus Christ. Jesus embraced the cross, for the joy set before Him, the joy of His coming bride. His marriage carriage is described as being made out of timber from Lebanon. Lebanon comes from the root word '*laban*,' which means 'to be white.' The posts are made of silver, which symbolizes redemption. Its base is gold, symbolizing wealth. The seat is purple, which is the symbolic color of royalty. And the interior is inlaid with love. Stunning!

This is a beautiful picture of our Bridegroom King and the eternal destiny that awaits His passionate lovers! "Rise up, Zion maidens, brides-to-be! Come and feast your eyes on this king as he passes in procession on his way to his wedding. This is the day filled with overwhelming joy- the day of his great gladness" (Song of Songs 3:11; TPT).

He is summoning the immature believers here to lay hold of their full inheritance and to let him lay hold of his full inheritance.

He is enticing young love, motivating us to push forward for more of him.

Chapter 4 greets us with the bridegroom's kindness, as he affirms to her how he sees her. He compares her hair to a flock of goats streaming down Mount Gilead. Hair is often symbolic in the Bible of our devotion to Christ. Interestingly, 'Mount Gilead' means 'hill of testimony.' Her devotion is streaming down the mountain, giving testimony to their love.

Then she declares something beautiful in verse 6, "I've made up my mind. Until the darkness disappears and the dawn has fully come, in spite of shadows and fears, I will go to the mountaintop with you- the mountain of suffering love and the hill of burning incense. Yes, I will be your bride" (TPT).

Her willingness to obey ravishes His heart. She hasn't physically done it yet, but she has set her face like flint and purposed to go, and this intention moves Him deeply. He willingly honors her intentions, even before the desired outcome is manifest. He affirms her first few steps towards obedience- declaring she is beautiful, acknowledging her affections. A legalistic spirit would not have done this, but the heart of a lover always will.

Mike Bickle wisely points out: "He does not motivate by shame, but He shares the joy of our progress each step of the way. God defines us by the cry in our heart. He does not define us by our struggles…He calls forth things that do not exist as though they did (Romans 4:17)."[30]

The Bridegroom responds by telling her she is ready. He tells her to descend from the crest of Amana so they can wage war together. The Dictionary of Scripture Proper Names by J.B. Jackson describes the 'Crest of Amana' as: "the realm where all God's promises are kept and realized. 'Amana' can also be translated 'a place of settled security.'"

This points us back to David and Goliath. David fought Goliath based on his covenant and history with the Lord. Here, the bridegroom is telling her to descend (lay hold of) God's promises, the place of settled security, so they can wage war together.

Then he says, "For you reach into my heart. With one flash of your eyes I am undone by your love, my beloved, my equal, my bride. You leave me breathless- I am overcome by merely a glance from your worshiping eyes, for you have stolen my heart. I am held hostage by your love and by the graces of righteousness shining upon you" (Song of Songs 4:9; TPT).

Your eyes of worship uncover His heart. The footnote in the Passion Translation says, "your loving eyes of worship have uncovered his heart and laid it bare, making him vulnerable to you."[31]

Wow! When you know you are loved, you can be vulnerable with people without the fear of rejection, and their response doesn't affect the posture of your heart. Jesus knows He is loved. The gaze of the Shulamite causes Him to be vulnerable to her. We think being vulnerable to people gives them power over us, but when you live loved, you have the capacity to be vulnerable without feeling personally threatened by that vulnerability.

As we discussed previously, the word 'staff' comes from a word that means 'to germinate, which produces shoots.' Verse 13 says, "Your shoots are an orchard of pomegranates." 'Pomegranate' comes from the Hebrew word '*ramam*' and means 'to be exalted, rise up, or to mount up.' In Jewish tradition, pomegranates are a symbol of love and fertility- pointing to an open heart, filled with passion for him. She is equating him to a shepherd who pastures his sheep in a way that always leads to love.

Nehemiah 11 talks about a place called En Rimmon, which means 'spring of a pomegranate." Interestingly, it is a city of Judah, mentioned after the exile, and was inhabited by the sons of Judah (Nehemiah 11:25,29). Everything He does points to love and causes love to spring up.

One of my favorite portions in this entire book comes from chapter 4:16-5:1. It has been my prayer anthem of late. It reads:

"Then may your awakening breath blow upon my life until I am fully yours. Breath upon me with your Spirit wind. Stir up the sweet spice of your life within me. Spare nothing as you make me your fruitful garden. Hold nothing back until I release your fragrance. Come walk with me as you walked with Adam in your paradise garden. Come taste the fruits of your life in me" (TPT).

She is asking him to completely transform her, from the inside out. Remember our friend the butterfly? She initially referred to her heart as '**my** garden,' but from here on out, she calls her heart '**His** garden.' She tells Him to spare nothing, leave no rock unturned, crucify every part of me, until my DNA is your DNA- until we are ONE. Her heart is now His garden, His new Eden.

This is the revelation she brought down from the crest of Amana, as she finally embraces that in order to become the bride, she must experience Calvary. She essentially declares, 'crucify me, until I no longer live but you live in me. Crucify me until we are one. Make me fully yours.'

She is so confident in their love; she no longer sees the cost of the cross. She will endure anything to lay hold of the promise of their great love together. The cross is the boldest example of love we can find, and it involves the entire trinity. The cross says, 'give me the things that hurt, the things that separate us, so I don't have to live another day without your love."

Up until this point, we hear the admonition not to awaken love until it is ready. It isn't until she embraces crucifixion herself that He says love can now be awakened. It is not about becoming good enough. He tells her throughout that she is lovely. But as we embrace crucifixion for ourselves, we cross-over. Now it's not just about our inheritance in Christ, but also about His inheritance in us. We willingly open ourselves to Him, that He may reap the fruit of His suffering love. And so will we.

It's important to understand we are simply worthy because He says we are. Nothing within our own merit will ever make us good enough. If it could, we wouldn't need Him. We were made for reciprocal love- reciprocal abiding. Love fights for freedom and it fights for free will. It must because God is love and His love is perfect.

The Shulamite isn't transformed because she works at trying to become clean. She is transformed as she grows in her understanding of how loved she is. The building revelations and growing capacity to receive His love, are what grow the fruit of transformation in her life and heart. From the inside out, His love invades every cave in her heart, fully transforming her. Fully restoring who she is and was always destined to be. Can you imagine what the world would be like if we all lived loved?

We don't strive to be loved. What does need to change though is our capacity to receive His love. When she finally realizes this, owning His love by owning His crucifixion, when she says this, then He says she is ready- because she has fully received His love. It isn't about becoming clean enough or worthy enough- that is the enslavement of a religious spirit. The religious spirit seeks to keep you bound, only looking at yourself, as Satan did. No, this is not our destiny.

This lie cheapens the cross. It parades itself around, proclaiming that Jesus paid the price for sin, but then we enslave ourselves, trying to become worthy enough for Him. When you do this, you are saying Jesus' death didn't buy your full redemption. It cheapens grace. Was Jesus not judged enough for sin?

To be clear, it is good to want to sanctify ourselves and remove the stumbling blocks that keep us from fullness. However, the motivation behind that effort cannot be based on the hopes it will curry more of His love or improve your worth to Him.

The cross is about the repayment for sin- the point of which is also about love. The true Christian journey, what the cross really points to, is learning to live loved. There is nothing you can do to increase or decrease His love for you. He pours out His affection without measure.

If you choose never to pursue sanctification, He will still love you with all that He is. However, it is good to pursue sanctification, because we want to look like Him, when it is birthed out of a response to His great love, and not in an effort to earn it.

Graham Cooke says, "There is nothing you can do to make Him love you more. There is also nothing you can do to make Him love you less. He loves you, because He loves you, because He loves you, because He loves you, because He loves you, because He loves you, because He loves you, because He loves, because He loves you, because He loves, because that is what He is like. It is His nature to love you. You will always be the Beloved. His love is unchanging. He loves you 100%. He won't love you any better when you become better. He loves all the way, all the time."

Love is the currency of Heaven. Love is the plumb line. Love is our inheritance. Living loved is who you are. Love is your covenant. Love is your past, present, and future. Loved is how He sees you. You are from a tribe called 'LOVE.' Love sets you free. Love holds you. Love surrounds you. You are His great love. It is who you are because it is who He is, and you are made in His image.

This is His bride. His overcomer. His warrior. She is worthy because He has paid the price for her. He is confident in her, as she brings Him good and not evil. He is not ashamed to display her to the world. He loves her and she loves him.

DARK (K)NIGHT OF THE SOUL
The Authority Of Love

The first four chapters of Song of Songs are all about the Shulamite's inheritance in the Bridegroom. From Chapter 4 onward, it is all about his inheritance in his bride. Chapter 5 begins with the bridegroom proclaiming she is his equal, his bride. He has come into his garden, her heart. He is no longer looking from the outside in, but he is all the way in. He is inhabiting her.

He has fully gathered all his spices from within her, she is now fully his. He compels everyone to feast and drink on his bride until they've had their fill. "…My life within her will become your feast" (Song of Songs 5:1; TPT).

After this, the Shulamite falls asleep and dreams of him, coming to her in the darkness of night. He pleads with her to open her heart to him deeper still, as his heaviness and tears are overwhelming. This points us back to Jesus in Gethsemane, as he prayed all night for us (John 17). And with this we understand he is testing her commitment- 'did you really mean what you said? Are you still all-in when things aren't going your way? When the night is long?'

She arises immediately, with her heart still yearning in love for him. She is fully committed. She is drenched in myrrh, pointing us to her commitment to him. She is willing to embrace death to herself, as his steadfast beloved.

This is the second time in the book where she experiences a withdrawing of His presence. The first was to provoke her away from disobedience. This time, it is because of her mature obedience. She is being tested. This is often referred to as 'the dark night of the soul,' where the ability to tangibly perceive his presence is gone. Will you hold steadfast in His love through this test?

"My beloved reached into me to unlock my heart. The core of my very being trembled at his touch...As I surrendered to him, I began to sense his fragrance- the fragrance of his suffering love! It was the sense of myrrh flowing all through me" (Song of Songs 5:4-5; TPT)!

The NASB says it this way, "My beloved **extended his hand** through the opening, and my feelings were aroused for him. I arose to open to my beloved; and my hands dripped with myrrh, and my fingers with liquid myrrh, on the handles of the bolt" (Song of Songs 5:4-5).

Remember 'Judah' means 'to extend the hand.' David extended the stone in his hand to slay Goliath. Jesus extended both of His hand on the cross to slay the death penalty requirement for sin. Here, Jesus is extending His hand into her heart. This time, **the extension rouses a sleeping giant instead of slaying one.** It rouses the giant of the Bride of Christ, crucified with Him.

I love that through the NASB translation, we can again see an allusion of Judah, where the Lord extends his hand into her heart. The word for 'his hand' in this passage comes from '*yadow*,' and while it means 'hand,' it can also mean 'to possess, power, strength, rule.' He reaches into her heart and she becomes his warrior of love.

The 'opening' or 'latch' as some translations say, is to open her heart. It comes from the word '*hahor*,' and means 'cave.' When he does this, when he extends his hand into the cave of her heart, she trembles; some translations say her heart pounded. This word in the original language is '*hamu*,' and one of the definitions for it is **'to roar.'**

He is the Lion of Tribe of Judah, and he has reached into her heart and unlocked the roar within her. We are one with His roar. He unleashes it from inside us. She can feel his fragrance, his suffering love flowing all the way through her, and then suddenly, he is gone. Every time I read this; I imagine the despair the disciples had as they watched Jesus hanging lifeless on the cross. They enjoyed the pleasure of being so close to him and then suddenly, everything changed, and they could not conceive what had happened.

Though He told them otherwise, I am sure they expected Him to mount-up a revolt, snap His fingers, and 'poof,' no more bad guys. Jesus hanging on a cross dead was not what they expected. Talk about hope deferred. Talk about the dark night of the soul.

"…if you find my beloved one, please tell him I endured all travails for him. I've been pierced through by love, and I will not be turned aside" (Song of Songs 5:8; TPT).

Next, the watchmen, the spiritual leaders 'wound' her and take away her covering. They reject her. In effect, she loses her place in ministry, her status is gone. Her ability to respond is being tested here. This shows us her willingness to obey in spite of their reproach. It reminds me of the Pharisees rejecting Jesus after He read Isaiah 61.

Will she rise up in offense and rebellion, perhaps even anger at him for 'leaving' her? Will she grow bitter at the spiritual leaders for rejecting her? Will she still be his even when he withholds the desires of her heart? Will she be his even though she cannot feel his presence? Will she still trust him even when her circumstances are disappointing? Will she remain steadfast in their love?

Beautifully, she responds to him with love, and the watchmen with humility, by asking for their help. She is all-in. She loves him with an intensity no circumstance can separate. He is her full devotion. Her only goal. Circumstances be what they will. She doesn't care if no one ever understands her. She will follow and obey Him.

After she endures a hard season of testing, the dark night of the soul, the king returns. He professes her beauty and her victory, likening her to a victorious army with banners. When an army returned in triumph from a battle, they displayed their banners in military procession. She has just defeated some major giants- the affairs and motivations of the heart, and the rejection of the watchmen.

Verse 6:2-3 say "My lover has gone down into his garden of delight, the place where his spices grow, to feast with those pure in heart. I know we shall find him there. He is within me- I am his garden of delight. **I have him fully and now he fully has me**" (TPT)!

Different translations give a varying description of him going to his garden, to pasture his flock and gather lilies. Either way, she now understands he is within her. He is dwelling within- she is his and he is hers. They are both all-in.

Then he responds, "O my beloved, you are lovely. When I see you in your beauty, I see a radiant city (the New Jerusalem) where we will dwell as one. More pleasing than any pleasure, more delightful than any delight, you have ravished my heart, stealing away my strength to resist you. Even hosts of angels stand in awe of you. Turn your eyes from me; I can't take it anymore! I can't resist the passion of these eyes that I adore. Overpowered by a glance, my ravished heart-undone. Held captive by your love, I am truly overcome! For your undying devotion to me is the most yielded sacrifice" (Song of Songs 6:4-5; TPT)!

The lovesick gaze of a believer who trusts Him wholeheartedly, in spite of difficulties, conquers His heart. When you love, regardless if things are going well or not, it highlights back to Him your level of devotion for Him. You are His warrior of love. Love is an ancient pathway- a new church faith. Our adoration for Him pierces time.

I love the footnote in The Passion Translation for verse 5, it reads, "The Hebrew word for 'overcome' is '*Rahab*.' Like the harlot who was chosen, favored, saved from Jericho's destruction, and included in the genealogy of Jesus, so you have 'overcome' his heart. No one would have thought Rahab would be so honored, and many have said that about you. You have overcome many things, but to overcome him is love's delight" (The Passion Translation, Second Edition, Page 1035).

At this, the Bridegroom responds: "Look at you now- arising as the dayspring of the dawn, fair as the shining moon. Bright and brilliant as the sun in all its strength. Astonishing to behold as a majestic army waving banners of victory" (Song of Songs 6:10; TPT).

He calls her the dayspring of the dawn. This is also a name for Jesus. Truly, they are one. He declares her in battle array, ready and empowered to go get the family back. To gather the exiles. The prodigals. This is the same mandate we read in Isaiah 61, Matthew 28:19, and Mark 16:15 (we will cover more on this in another chapter). This is our mission, should we choose to accept it.

In verse 11, she decides to go down into the valley, the garden, to see if the vines are budding. 'Vines' come from an unused root word meaning 'to bend; or twining, especially the grape vine tree.' 'Twining' can be defined as 'twisting; winding; coiling; embracing; climbing by winding about a support.'[32] In other words, is new life breaking forth? Are hearts blooming in love, and awakening to him? Are they yearning for more of him? Do they trust him yet?

Without realizing it, she says her desire sets her among the chariots of her people. Her passion sets her, literally appoints her, among the chariots of her noble people. 'Among the chariots' is derived from the root word '*rakab*,' which means 'to mount and ride, to lead.' 'Noble' is derived from the root word '*nadab*,' and the primitive root means 'offer freely, to willingly offer yourself, to volunteer as a soldier.' 'People' is derived from a primitive root word that means 'to associate; by implication, to overshadow (by huddling together)- become dim, hide.' Simplified, her passionate desire of love has, unbeknownst to her, appointed her to mount and ride, to lead a people who have freely come, though they are dark, to get the exiles back.

The brides-to-be plead with her to come back, to dance for them as they gaze on her beauty. The expression, 'that we may gaze upon you' comes from the word *'chazah,'* which means 'to see, behold, prophesy.' A primitive root which means 'to have a vision.' It's as if they are wanting to understand her better so they can see the blueprint of how to become his radiant bride.

'Dancing' comes from the root word *'chuwl,'* which means 'to dance, make to bring forth.' 'Of Mahanaim' comes from the word *'machaneh,'* which means 'two camps; an encampment, army camp, host.' In Genesis 32:1 we read, "Now as Jacob went on his way, the angels of God met him. Jacob said when he saw them, "This is God's camp." So he named that place Mahanaim."

In other words, it is the place where two camps of angels abide. She is actively engaged with the hosts of heaven and the brides-to-be want the manual on how to get 'there.'

In Chapter 7 the bridegroom is declaring the beauty of his bride and it is ripe with military symbolism. He says her hips are curvy like jewels and her navel is round like a goblet. The word for 'curves' comes from a root word *'chamaq,'* which means 'to turn away, withdraw self.' The reference to hips comes from the word *'yarek,'* which means 'thigh, shaft.' It is a euphemism for a shank, the place where a sword is drawn. When he compares these things to jewels, it is a word play for being polished. In other words, she is polished, proficient, at turning away evil with the sword. She is a polished warrior.

The reference to her navel like a round goblet which never lacks mixed wine, is also beautifully poetic. 'Navel' is derived from the word *'shor,'* and literally means 'umbilical cord.' Figuratively, it is used to describe the center of strength. The goblet of mixed wine is a reference to tempered wine. Glass is tempered to remove impurities, thereby making it much stronger than normal glass, and able to withstand great heat. So, he is saying she is strong at her core because she has been tempered, the impurities (foxes) have been removed. the power of his blood and spirit flow through her. She can withstand the heat of trials.

The reference to her belly like 'a heap of wheat fenced about with lilies' (verse 2) also tells us a lot. 'Belly' comes from a word that means 'body, womb.' 'Wheat' is derived from a word that means 'to spice, ripen, embalm, put forth.' We have already discussed lilies are a symbol of purity. He is saying here that she nurtures those in her care, with the purity she imparts to them. She is a spiritual mother to all who seek her.

He continues, describing her as a great watchtower, a shining light on a hill, a stronghold of refreshment for others, a tower of discernment in the face of opposition, the head over the garden- full of wisdom and virtue. He declares the royalty permeating from her imprisons his affections. Her devotion holds him hostage.

"...Love has become the greatest. You stand in victory above the rest, stately and secure as you share with me your vineyard of love. Now I decree, I will ascend and arise. I will take hold of you with my power, possessing every part of my fruitful bride.... Your kisses of love (her transformation) awaken even the lips of sleeping ones" (Songs of Songs 7:6-9; TPT).

She responds back to him (7:10-12), "Now I know that I am filled with my beloved and his desires are fulfilled in me. Come away, my lover. Come with me to the faraway fields. We will run away together to the forgotten places and show them redeeming love. Let us arise and run to the vineyards of your people and see if the budding vines of love are now in full bloom. We will discover if their passion is awakened. There I will display my love for you" (TPT).

This can be said another way – lets go get Your brides-to be! Let's capture more of Your inheritance!

In John 14:12, Jesus says, "I tell you the truth, anyone who believes in me will do the same works I have done, and even greater works, because I am going to be with the Father" (NLT).

I have always heard this passage taught as we will do even greater miracles than Jesus did. It wasn't until recently I really started to think about that. Is it actually possible to do greater miracles than Jesus did? John 21:25 tells us there would not be enough books in the world to contain all the miracles that Jesus performed. As I started to seek the Holy Spirit about this passage, He began to speak to me about the Bride of Christ.

The Greek word for 'greater' in this passage is the word '*megas*.' Megas means 'larger, magnitude, greatness of size, magnify, to extol.' It speaks of multiplication. In other words, what Jesus is saying to us in John 14:12 is this: 'What I did on earth, I did as one man. You will do greater works than Me because you will do them as my army- My triumphant bride.'

Chapter 8 begins with the Shulamite petitioning for more strength and depth- for boldness in public ministry and in their partnership, to make their union abundantly known. With this, he affirms her, professing, "...Look at her now! She arises out of her desert, clinging to her beloved..." (Song of Songs 8:5; TPT).

When I have read this verse in the past, I have always pictured her as utterly exhausted, barely surviving the testing she had endured, and thus the need for 'leaning' or 'clinging' to her beloved. I was wrong. This word comes from a primitive word that means 'to recline.' In other words, she is so at rest in their love, so confident in it- no trial is going to shake her from it. The 'foxes' of chapter two are long gone. The disposition of the watchmen is inconsequential to her. Nothing shakes her devotion.

God's highest calling for us is to be transformed into Christlikeness. The Bible tells us that only the overcomers who have been conformed to Christlikeness will be chosen to rule and reign with Christ on the highest levels of responsibility, for eternity.

The heavenly reward is worth the temporary, earthly sacrifice it costs us. The apostle Paul tells us it pales in comparison.

To reiterate what I said in the Introduction, living loved is the greatest thing we could hope to accomplish in this life. It wrecks violence on the enemy and empowers an otherwise sleeping giant- His bride. Love is the currency of heaven.

Heidi Baker says, "You have no authority where you have no love."

"Fasten me upon your heart as a seal of fire forevermore. This living, consuming flame will seal you as my prisoner of love. My passion is stronger than the chains of death and the grave, all consuming as the very flashes of fire from the burning heart of God. Place this fierce, unrelenting fire over your entire being" (Song of Songs 8:6; TPT).

He invites her to receive the seal of fire upon her heart, and to walk with Him in holy, bold, jealous love. 'Seal' comes from the word '*kahowtam*,' and means 'seal or signet-ring.' Historically, signet-rings were often used as an instrument to sign official documents. The mark(s) on the ring were specific to point to the identity of the wearer. From this we learn, they will never be separated again. She will never again know a moment without Him.

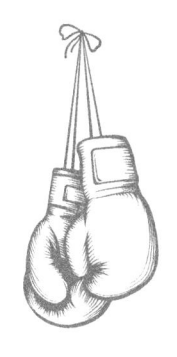

THE ENDGAME
Being An Ambassador For Christ

Covenant is a roadmap for us, defining God's eternal faithfulness and devotion to us. We spent the first portion of this book discussing the power of identity and dissecting old covenant battles and strategies. It outlined for us the purpose and power of understanding covenant, and how to use our covenant promises as a weapon against our external adversary.

We spent the second portion of this book dissecting Song of Songs. A book that is also about the power of identity and covenant. All with the explicit purpose of fighting the enemies within, conquering our heartland, and establishing an eternal covenant of love. As the Shulamite grew in her ability to trust his love, their covenant relationship flourished. Trust is built on covenant.

We will spend the last section of this book discussing where we go from here. What is our mandate now as the Bride of Christ? What is our roadmap for advancing His kingdom? And how do we share His all-consuming love with a world that doesn't even know they're desperate for it?

We know the enemy only comes to fight, but Jesus defeated him on the cross and then handed us the keys to enforce that victory. Why then does the enemy persist? Everything Satan does is to inhibit love. Satan was cast out of heaven and Jesus defeated him on the cross, making the forever payment for our sins. Remember, battles are not about circumstances. Battle are about trust, and trust is built on covenant.

God is not focused on the enemy because He has defeated him. God is not focused on our sin because Jesus paid an eternal price for it. From the Lord's standpoint then, the only battle that remains, is the battle for your heart- for your love. Love is the last battle frontier. And when you know you're loved; Satan knows nothing will be able to stop you.

You can't know you're loved until you know you can trust Him. And you can't trust Him until you know you're loved. This is the great dance of our time- going from glory to glory, as we grow in trusting love. It is meant to saturate the deepness within your humanity until every part of you is kissed by love.

Your identity is LOVED. Your inheritance is LOVE. You belong to a tribe called 'LOVE.' Your destiny is LOVE. Everything God does is motivated by love. Everything you face in life should be faced from the posture of being loved. All of heaven is fighting a battle for your heart. We are in a war over love.

I had a dream recently I was in a battle, running head-on towards five ferocious grizzly bears- all of this unfolding at a campground. As I was running towards the grizzly bears to fight, I suddenly realized how big they were, and I recognized I was fairly exposed on the open ground. And, I was running alone.

In the dream I knew that in order to gain victory on them, I needed to get up higher and fight them from an elevated advantage. I jumped on top of a nearby truck-camper for some altitude, and to figure out what I needed to do next. From this vantage point they looked much smaller in size and easier to defeat, which I was thankful for.

As I stood on top of the camper, I observed four of the grizzly bears standing off to the left side in a row, all watching the fifth grizzly bear who was devouring a woman's womb. As I was watching the woman, who was screaming out in agony over what was happening to her womb, I was simultaneously trying to figure out the best way I could help her.

In this moment, I suddenly realized I was holding a cell phone. My mom was on the line, yet her words were the Lord's. Somehow in the dream, I knew I was talking to both of them. I said, "Mom, I need to let you go! I have to try and help this woman! Is there anything you want me to tell her?"

The earnest response: "Yes! Tell her God loves her!"

That was the end of the dream. As I have prayed about the interpretation of this dream, I believe the Lord is speaking some very clear things through it. These five grizzly bears clearly run together as evil brothers in arms, and I believe they represent some of the strongholds in America right now. They have been camped out in our land, stealing our inheritance, for far too long. In fact, 'camped' in Hebrew is the word *'wayyahanu'* and can mean 'to lay siege against, or to encamp with hostile purpose' (Joshua 10:5).

I believe the bear devouring the woman's womb is symbolic of abortion. It was odd to me in the dream that the other four bears were lined up watching this bear. As I prayed about this, I felt a sense in the spirit of a domino effect. Almost as if the defeat of this abortive bear, would lead to a domino effect of the defeat of the other four, as these forces of evil are influenced by each other. And the order they were established in, happened in a domino effect, as evil was built upon evil.

Merriam-Webster defines 'domino effect' as: 'a cumulative effect produced when one event initiates a succession of similar events.'[33] Likewise is the 'domino theory' which states that if one act or event is allowed to take place, a series of similar acts or events will follow.

Climbing on top of the camper, putting in proper perspective the size of the bears, also spoke a lot to me. Psalm 24 speaks about warfare that is waged by ascending the holy hill or mountain of the Lord. It provides a vantage point that cannot be obtained through ground warfare. When we get up higher, everything falls into proper perspective, and we are able to advance as we now see the whole picture. When we 'come up higher,' we are positioned to hear the council of heaven.

Being on the call with my mom and her response speaks a lot to me, especially after what we have covered with Caleb, David and Goliath, and the Lion of Judah. Caleb, whose name means 'wholehearted,' David, whose name means 'beloved,' and Jesus, whose name means 'to deliver or rescue, savior.' Each of them slayed giants by being who and what God had made them to be.

I believe part of this phone call represented an alignment of generations and drawing on our DNA and heritage as the Beloved of God. I also think it's important to point out that the only advice I received was to speak about His love. I was not given any instructions about the enemy or how to fight off the bears, or even to address the woman's sin.

As I thought about this, I realized that God was more concerned the woman knew He loved her, than He was about the giants or her sin. He didn't instruct me to command her to repent. He didn't judge or condemn her. He simply wanted her to know she was loved. Does this offend you?

We need to be careful we don't become so justice oriented, that we steamroll Grace. This battle is not about our desired outcome or our self-righteousness. It's about His love. God isn't focused on the enemy because Jesus has already defeated him. God isn't focused on our sin because Jesus already paid for it. God is focused on making His love known, because from His standpoint, that's the only battle that remains. The battle for our hearts.

Jeremiah 31:3 says, "The Lord appeared to him from afar, saying, 'I have loved you with an everlasting love; therefore I have drawn you with lovingkindness.'" This passage speaks of a love that has no beginning and no end. His love is an eternal flame that never burns out.

I can also sense from the call, the Lord commissioning me to share my testimony with this giant. My life truly is a walking testimony, a trophy of God's miraculous grace. Like David, my name also means 'beloved.' I want to share part of my journey with you now.

I did not grow up in church. We were the typical sports family, spending every weekend at the ballfield. For a brief period though, when I was ten years old, my family attended a southern Baptist church near our house. I usually sat through service bored, wondering what I would eat for lunch. At the end of one of the services, the pastor gave what I now know is an altar call. When I heard him say the name 'Jesus,' I began to cry uncontrollably.

I didn't have much context for what was going on, but I knew I needed this Jesus guy. I pushed through the aisle I was in, marched up front to the stage, and told the pastor I wanted this Jesus. He led me in the sinner's prayer and a few months later I was baptized at a pool.

However, with no real underpinning, I found myself at the age of twenty-one, having wandered very far from anything I ever thought my life would look like. I had made some terrible decisions leading me to my absolute rock bottom. Ashamed at who I had become and the choices I had made, I decided I didn't need to live anymore.

As I sat on my bathroom floor at 3am, trying the figure out how I could take my own life without leaving a huge mess for my mom to clean up, while also contemplating if committing suicide would mean a one-way ticket to hell or not, I heard the audible voice of God: "HAVE YOU HAD ENOUGH YET?"

I sat there in silence, scared, looking around the bathroom, suddenly not sure what was going on as I lived alone in my apartment. Then I heard it again: "HAVE YOU HAD ENOUGH YET?"

Up to this point in my life I had never heard the audible voice of God and never knew it was even a possibility. Yet somehow, I knew. I knew He was talking to me. What followed next was twenty-one years' worth of word vomit. Hurt, rejection, regret, and pain all came spewing out of my mouth in anger at God.

"Where have you been?!?! Where were you when I felt rejected? Alone? Unloved? Where were you when it felt like nobody wanted me? Where were you all those years' I felt invisible and misunderstood? Where were you when she molested me and caged me? Where were you when he abused and isolated me? And where were you, just hours ago, when I made the worst decision of my life and aborted my baby? Where were you?!"

As I said, 'word vomit.' Blaming the Lord for every bad thing in my life. I unloaded until I had nothing left to say. Every awful thing that had ever been done to me and every poor choice I had ever made. All of it, tabled. Just me, the Lord, and all my 'stuff.'

"HAVE YOU HAD ENOUGH YET?" He persisted.

I sat in silence for a moment as everything sank in. I began to realize what the Lord was actually asking me: "Have you had enough of doing things your way and racing through life without me? Look where it's gotten you. Is this really what you want because it's not what I want for you? I miss you and I still love you, even in spite of all of this! Have you had enough of living without knowing my love?"

As I realized this, I found myself quickly becoming aware of His overwhelming grace. I felt myself succumbing as I was slowly realizing the heart behind what He was asking. As my white knuckling of the pain, regret, and anger were weakening, I could feel desperation taking its place. This overwhelming sense of knowing I needed Him began to rush my being and I started to panic.

Desperate He might quickly change His mind, I managed to blurt out, "Lord, if it's not too late for me, if you will just let me scrub the toilets in Heaven, I will serve you with everything I've got for the rest of my life! Please don't leave me! I need you!"

And I sat puddled on the floor as I cried to God, letting my tears be the words I could no longer articulate for the gravity of the moment. Peace eventually flushed my heart and for the first time in as long as I could remember, I had hope and felt seen. I mean truly seen. The good, the bad, and the ugly – and yet somehow, He was still choosing me.

It is important to note that I have since apologized to the Lord for spewing word vomit on Him. The Lord is not the source of our pain- either caused by others or our own poor choices.

I shared all of that to lay a foundation for what I am about to share next. Let's get back to the grizzly bears, and the advice from my mom to tell the woman God loved her.

My name means 'beloved' in English, and as I've shared already, my own life is stained with the sin of abortion. Thankfully, my story and life didn't end there. The advice from my mom to tell the woman in the dream that God loves her, in the midst of her womb being devoured, highlighted back to me my own testimony, even my own name and DNA. I hope what I share next from my staff, slings a hard stone at this giant, and releases healing for anyone who needs it.

It was hours after I aborted my baby, in the darkest and ugliest moment of my life, that the Lord showed me His incredible love. He met me in my darkest moment of pain and made His love known to me by tangibly making Himself known to me. By letting me know that He still saw me and still wanted me. As I've shared, my name means 'beloved,' and I have a testimony with God, where He has fully and tangibly shown His love and mercy to me.

When I rededicated my life to the Lord, I needed a lot of inner healing. Seeking healing for my abortion, a friend urged me to pray and ask the Lord to bring healing to this area of my life and even to ask Him to show me where my baby was. I thought this was a great idea and honestly, I had nothing to lose by following through on it.

Apparently, heaven had been waiting for this appointed time, because as soon as I prayed, I immediately had a vision. In the vision, I was looking out over a meadow full of children everywhere. They were running around playing and laughing. At the center of it all was Jesus. Children were hanging on Him, chasing Him around, laughing with Him. His tenderness with them was overwhelming.

My gaze was then drawn to a little girl with blonde hair, who looked to be about the age my child would have been if she'd been alive. Somehow, I knew she was mine and I couldn't take my eyes off her. I was so excited to learn my baby was a girl. Honestly, just to know anything about my baby was a gift to me. Then I broke down and started crying as the peace of knowing my baby was with Jesus flooded my heart- starting to heal the Grand Canyon of hurt and regret in my life over this decision I had made.

I asked the Lord in the vision if I could see her closer and, as if on cue, Jesus held her hand and walked her across the meadow to me. With her standing before me, all I could do in the vision was cry and tell her how sorry I was- asking her to forgive me for what I had done to her. I sat on the grass holding her in the vision, wishing I could have her back but knowing she was no longer mine. She belonged to Jesus now and I was so grateful for His mercy and love to allow me this opportunity. As I watched my little girl and Jesus walk back to the meadow with all the other children, I asked the Father what He had named her.

"ABIGAIL."

'Abigail' is a Hebrew name and it means, 'my father's joy.' That brought me to tears as I imagined the absolute joy they now had for each other. I cried for some time following that vision, and even still when I think back on the goodness of God to allow me that opportunity. To meet my baby and to know she is with Jesus has brought more healing than you can possibly imagine.

I will never not regret the awful decision I made to abort her. There isn't a day that goes by that I don't think about her, miss her, or long to hold her. That ache is never going to leave, as there is a part of me literally missing from this world. This gift of healing the Lord gave me, however, has given me so much hope and I treasure it deeply. This encounter is carved on my staff. It is a testimony of God's healing love and grace to me, in the midst of giant darkness.

Men and women everywhere need to know the truth about abortion, from someone who has walked through it. They need to know the depth of hurt that follows. There is a lot of misinformation, funded by pro-abortion camps, that would lead people to believe there are no adverse mental health traumas that follow an abortion. This is a lie and here's the reason why: "We have a saying in the world of therapy. 'Secrets kill.' Thus is the path of many women after abortion. Don't talk. Don't feel, keep the secret." Trudy M. Johnson, M.A., LMFT

This was true for me. It was hours after my abortion that I was plotting my suicide. And I had resolved to tell no one. Feeling buried in my shame, alone, with no way out. But, God.

We will never see a well-rounded truthful analysis on post-abortive trauma because the majority of women are not willing to discuss it, with anyone. If you have had an abortion, or even just experienced the loss of a miscarriage; you need to know your baby is with Jesus. Ask Him to give you a vision for your little one. Ask Him what He has named your little one.

If you have had an abortion, you need to know the Lord has an abundance of grace for you. You need to know He has healing in His wings, waiting to be poured out for you. You need to know He is waiting for you to bring your hurt to Him. You need to know He is a good father. Most importantly, you need to know HE LOVES YOU.

SCOTOPLO
Accosting The Darkness

I was having a dream one night in which I was simply studying the spelling of a word. It was pitch black in the dream and the word was in bold white letters. That's it, nothing fancy. I carefully studied each letter of the word, somehow knowing in the dream the Lord wanted me to remember the spelling when I awoke.

I repeated the spelling out loud in the dream and then said, "Ok, Lord, I think I've got it."

As soon as I said that, I awoke from the dream. Now awake, but still feeling the same intensity I had in the dream, I immediately wrote the word down so I would not forget the exact spelling. I had never heard the word before and wasn't even sure if it was a real word.

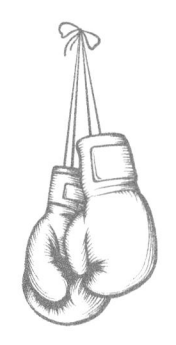

'*S C O T O P L O*'

An internet search of the word, at the time, thankfully only yielded 3 results in English. With this, I knew the exact meaning 'night vision.' Further confirmed by the dream being pitch black and only the letters in white. The logical next step for me was to ask, "how does night vision work?"

Your eyes contain two types of photoreceptor cells in the retina – rod cells and cone cells. These cells absorb light and convert the light through a process that allows you to have vision in the presence of light, whether bright or dim. Rod cells function in low light and cone cells function in bright light.

Psalm 23:4 says, "Even though I walk through the **darkest valley**, I will fear no evil, for you are with me; your **rod** and your staff, they comfort me."

Did you catch that? Science tells us rod cells are what allow our eyes to see in dim light. Psalm 23 says when we walk through the darkest valley…His rod and staff comfort us.

As we've discussed previously, shepherds always carried two sticks with them when they were looking after sheep. A shorter stick, called a 'rod,' was used to fight off wild dogs and other predators. The other stick they carried was called a 'staff.' The staff was usually longer than the rod and had a curved hook at one end. The staff was used to lead the sheep, as well as to rescue them when they wandered where they shouldn't or got stuck. They could wrap the hook around the sheep's neck and pull it off a dangerous cliff, out of a sinkhole or mud pit, or help redirect the sheep whenever needed.

The words "of the shadow of death" come from the word '*salmawet*', meaning 'death-shadow, deep darkness, extreme danger, or literally a place of the dead.' Jesus tells us in John 16:33 that we will have trouble in this life. We will face persecution, endure affliction, experience distress, walk through tribulation, bear great pressure, etc. Jesus tells us however, to have courage, to be bold and of good cheer because He has overcome the world.

The words "Your rod" come from the word '*sibteka*,' meaning 'rod, staff, scepter (mark of authority), clan, tribe, branch, offshoot.' The word 'staff' comes from the word '*umisanteka*.' It means 'support of every kind, protector, sustenance.'

The words "comfort me" come from the word '*yenahamuni*,' meaning 'to be sorry, repent, regret, be comforted.' Sometimes we find ourselves in darkness because we have done something foolish and need to be led to repentance. Other times we find ourselves in trouble simply because we live in a fallen world and need comfort and nourishment from Him.

Psalm 23:4 is a beautiful reminder to us that when we find ourselves in deep darkness, His rod- a literal scepter of authority, is with us to chase away the evil that has come against us. His staff is with us to help restore us to His ways. He is with us to help us see and find our way through. He promises to comfort us and to lead us to repentance.

"God, all at once you turned on a floodlight for me! You are the revelation-light in my darkness, and in your brightness I can see the path ahead. With you as my strength I can crush an enemy horde, advancing through every stronghold that stands in front of me. What a God you are! Your path for me has been perfect! All your promises have proven true. What a secure shelter for all those who turn to hide themselves in you! You are the wrap-around God giving grace to me" (Psalm 18:28-30; TPT).

"The people who were sitting in darkness saw a great light, and those who were sitting in the land and shadow of death, upon them a light dawned" (Matthew 4:16). Some translations use the words 'living in darkness,' instead of sitting. The original word can mean both, and even 'to dwell or abide.'

When you find yourself in darkness or surrounded by the shadow of death, don't live there. Don't set-up camp and let it become your identity. We are meant to keep moving. Just keep walking, just keep pushing. Don't stop and don't give up. His name, the essence of who He is, accosts darkness. Jesus says in John 8:12, "…'I am the Light of the world; he who follows Me will not walk in the darkness but will have the Light of life." When we walk with Jesus, His light radiates our atmosphere, chasing away darkness.

Isaiah 60:1-3 tells us, "Arise, shine; for your light has come, and the glory of the Lord has risen upon you. For behold, darkness will cover the earth and deep darkness the peoples; but the Lord will rise upon you and His glory will appear upon you. Nations will come to your light, and kings to the brightness of your rising."

The very glory of Jesus now rests on us and shines through us. We are meant to radiate His presence. To infuse our surroundings with His revelation light, as nations and kings will be drawn to it.

"Christ in you, the hope of glory" (Colossians 1:27).

I have started asking the Lord for prophetic scotoplo (night vision). For the supernatural ability to see well in the night; to see the enemies plans exposed and dead on arrival. What if we started praying for the Cartel? Not just for their plans to be exposed, but for the prophetic utterance to declare light into the darkness. What if we lived as though we actually believed we were light in the dark?

In a few weeks I will be moving to a new home. Every time we move, I search the address on familywatchdog.us. It's a free service that shows you sex offenders in your proximity and lists their address, photo, and name. There are three near the neighborhood of my new home. I have already started to pray light into their darkness. I am asking the Lord for scriptures, prophetic words, and words of knowledge for them. I have every intention of taking new territory for Jesus when I move. I have every intention of being light in the midst of darkness. His crucifixion paid for this to be our reality.

"To open their eyes so that they may turn from darkness to light and from the dominion of Satan to God, that they may receive forgiveness of sins and an inheritance among those who have been sanctified by faith in Me" (Acts 26:18).

His crucifixion was so powerful, the Apostle Paul declared he sought to know nothing in life but Jesus Christ and Him crucified. We can see more of Jesus' mandate and destiny on earth as we read Isaiah 61:

> "The Spirit of the Lord God is upon me, because the Lord has anointed me to bring good news to the afflicted; He has sent me to bind up the brokenhearted, to proclaim liberty to captives and freedom to prisoners (release from darkness); to proclaim

the favorable year of the Lord and the day of vengeance of our God; to comfort all who mourn, to grant those who mourn in Zion, giving them a garland instead of ashes, the oil of gladness instead of mourning, the mantle of praise instead of a spirit of fainting.

So they will be called oaks of righteousness, the planting of the Lord, that He may be glorified. Then they will rebuild the ancient ruins, they will raise up the former devastations; and they will repair the ruined cities, the desolations of many generations. Strangers will stand and pasture your flocks, and foreigners will be your farmers and your vinedressers. But you will be called the priests of the Lord; you will be spoken of as ministers of our God. You will eat the wealth of nations, and in their riches you will boast. Instead of your shame you will have a double portion, and instead of humiliation they will shout for joy over their portion. Therefore, they will possess a double portion in their land, everlasting joy will be theirs. For I, the Lord, love justice, I hate robbery in the burnt offering; and I will faithfully give them their recompense and make an everlasting covenant with them. Then their offspring will be known among the nations, and their descendants in the midst of the peoples. All who see them will recognize them because they are the offspring whom the Lord has blessed. I will rejoice greatly in the Lord, my soul will exult in my God; for He has clothed me with garments of salvation, He has wrapped me with a robe of righteousness, as a bridegroom decks himself with a garland, and

> as a bride adorns herself with her jewels. For as the earth brings forth its sprouts (shoots), and as a garden causes the things sown in it to spring up, so the Lord God will cause righteousness and praise to spring up before all the nations."

Isaiah 61:1 tells us the spirit of the Lord is upon him (Jesus) to, among other things, release prisoners from darkness. When you look this passage up in the original language, it comes from the word *'qowah,'* which means to "open the eyes wide." Additionally, Isaiah 61:3 speaks of a mantle of praise in exchange for a spirit of despair. 'Despair' in this passage comes from the original language word *'kehah,'* meaning 'dim, dull, colorless, dark, faint.' He came to pierce the darkness. To cut through the shroud. To open the eyes.

Verse 4 reads, 'they will rebuild.' This comes from the original word *'ubanu.'* One of the main definitions of this word is in reference to 'establishing a family, restoring exiles, or being built up as a childless wife would be by becoming a mother of a family.'

'The ancient ruins,' is a translation of two words: *'owlam'* and *'harebowt.'* *'Owlam'* is defined as 'everlasting, perpetual, old, futurity, continuous existence, eternity.' *'Harebowt'* is defined as 'a place of desolation and ruin.'

What is the Lord saying here? Jesus was anointed to set prisoner's free, to repair the breech, to restore the places of desolation- all with the explicit purpose of reestablishing God's family. Jesus, laying hold of all time and eternity, came to restore the exiles and re-establish the Father's family. He came to conquer death in order to get God's family back. We are part of that mission.

"*Ekklesia*" (ecclesia) is the Greek word for church, though it means so much more than that. *'Ekklesia'* is a governmental term, more appropriately meaning 'legislative assembly or selected ones.' It is not a religious term, but a governmental one. It is used to define a group of people, summoned together to govern the affairs of a city.

As such, when Jesus uses this term, He is granting the keys of governmental authority in His kingdom, to the church. There is absolutely no force of darkness that can stop the awakened church Jesus is building- His triumphant bride.

In Matthew 16:18, Jesus is talking to Peter, and He tells him that 'upon this rock I will build My church; and the gates of Hades will not overpower it. Peter's name means 'rock.' 'Build' in this passage comes from the Greek word '*oikodomeo*,' which is derived from two Greek words: '*oikos*' and '*doma*.' '*Oikos*' is used to describe descendants, families, and homes. '*Doma*' is used to describe the roof of a house.

It seems, from dissecting this chapter, that Jesus isn't just talking about constructing a building. But more appropriately, descendants. He wants to establish a lineage, build a family. His church isn't a structure, it's a people.

"…and this truth of who I am will be the bedrock foundation on which I will build my church- my legislative assembly, and the power of death will not be able to overpower it! I will give you the keys of heaven's kingdom realm to forbid on earth that which is forbidden in heaven and to release on earth that which is released in heaven" (Matthew 16:18-19).

Isaiah 61:8 says, "For I, the Lord, love justice, I hate robbery in the burnt offering; and I will faithfully give them their recompense and make an everlasting covenant with them." The word 'covenant' in this passage comes from the word '*berith*.' Not only does this word mean 'covenant,' it also means 'confederacy.' A confederacy is an alliance of people, formed for an illicit purpose. When this word is used in reference between people, it is translated as: 'a treaty, alliance, constitution, or agreement.' When it is used between God and man, it is translated as: 'covenant, with divine ordinance of signs.'

As the Ekklesia of God, we are meant to be in alliance with one another, as we jealously pursue the covenants of the Lord, which is meant to be followed by a 'divine ordinance of signs.' We are called out (ekklesia) from the world and into His body, to rule and reign. To bring heaven to earth.

Psalm 115:16 says, 'The heavens belong to our God; they are his alone, but he has given us the earth and put us in charge" (TPT).

In reference to Jesus, Acts 4:28-31 says, "They did to Him all that Your purpose and will had determined, according to the destiny You had marked out for Him. So now, Lord, listen to their threats to harm us. Empower us, as your servants, to speak the word of God freely and courageously. Stretch out your hand of power through us to heal, and to move in signs and wonders by the name of Your holy Son, Jesus! At that moment the earth shook beneath them, causing the building they were in to begin to tremble. Each one of them was filled with the Holy Spirit, and they proclaimed the word of God with unrestrained boldness" (TPT).

'Boldness' in this passage comes from the word *'parresia.'* The footnote in The Passion Translation says this about *'parresia:'* "…The person who speaks with *parresia* will say everything that is on his mind with no restraint, flowing out of his heart with confidence. In involves being frank and honest, hiding nothing and speaking directly to the heart…It refers to speech that is not tailored to make everyone happy but to speak the truth, in spite of what that may cost."[34]

Jesus tells us in Matthew 28:18 that all authority has been given to Him and consequently commands us in verse 19 to, "go therefore and make disciples of all nations." The Hebrew word for 'go' in this verse, is the word *'poreuomai.'* While this word is often used in reference to 'traveling, journeying, and going;' it is also used in Hebrew, metaphorically, as a reference to 'dying.'

We see this as true when we read Luke 22:22, where Jesus says, "The Son of Man must now 'go' where he will be sacrificed" (TPT). With this in mind, we better understand what Jesus is commanding in Matthew 28:19. He is commanding us to identify with His death, to lay aside the old man, and put on His resurrection power. He is telling us to make known His victorious spectacle over death, to restore the exiles of His family, therefore making disciples. He is telling us to be His ekklesia, His authority in the earth.

Christ made it possible for us to be children of God again, through His crucifixion. He is essentially saying to us here, 'Now that I have done that, identify with me, or literally clothe yourself with who I am by wearing my authority as your own, and go get the family back from the grave of darkness.'

We see this evidenced further in Mark 16:15 when Jesus says, "go into all the world and preach the gospel to all creation." The word used for 'creation' in this verse is the Greek word '*kitzo*,' and it is used in reference to 'the act of founding, creating, establishing, and building- with family in mind.'

When you put Isaiah 61, Matthew 16:18, Matthew 28:19 and Mark 16:15 together, we can clearly see that Jesus is commanding us to reestablish or rebuild His family, His church body, and enforce His domain in the earth. He is commanding us to restore things to the order God had originally intended, now made possible through the crucifixion of Christ.

"I have been crucified with Christ; and it is no longer I who live, but Christ lives in me; and the life which I now live in the flesh I live by faith in the Son of God, who loved me and gave Himself up for me" (Galatians 2:20).

Romans 7:4 explains that we were made to die to the Law through the body of Christ, so that we may be joined to Him and bear fruit. 'Bearing fruit' in this passage is a reference to the Greek word '*karpophoresomen*,' derived from the word '*karpophoros*,' which means 'to be fertile.' Fertility is always about family, always about producing literal or spiritual sons and daughters. This echoes in a new way what I said previously; Christ died in our place so that we could be joined back to Him in union and bear offspring (reestablish the exiles) into God's family.

"But because of His great love for us, God, who is rich in mercy, made us alive with Christ, even when we were dead in our trespasses.

It is by grace you have been saved! And God raises us up with Christ and seated us with Him in the heavenly realms in Christ Jesus, in order that in the coming ages He might display the surpassing riches of His grace, demonstrated by His kindness to us in Christ Jesus" (Ephesians 2:4-7; Berean Study Bible).

Revelation 12 tells us we overcome the enemy by the blood of the Lamb. His church- His bride, is meant to be a legislative force on the earth; enforcing His governmental rule- on earth as it is in Heaven. All with the intention of God getting His kids back.

"Your kingdom come. Your will be done, on earth as it is in heaven" (Matthew 6:10).

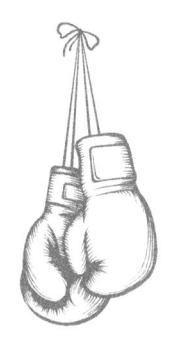

CAGED NO MORE
Restoring The Former Desolations

The same day I woke up from the Scotoplo dream, something bizarre happened to my cellphone. I reached for my phone to see what time it was, and on the locked display of my phone were the words "Caged No More," as if I had been watching or listening to something with that title. It was so bizarre, I took a screenshot, so I could confirm it had actually happened and wasn't just a vision.

Having no idea what this was, as I was currently not using or watching my phone, I decided to search the internet for "Caged No More." I discovered it was a movie about human trafficking. In the film, the father owes a substantial amount of money to drug dealers. Unable to pay his debt, he sells both his daughters into sex slavery in exchange for money to pay his drug debt. The daughters find themselves in literal slavery as a result of the sin of their father.

Through a series of events, a caretaker for the girls calls on a family member to help with a rescue attempt to recover the girls. It is a beautiful example of a kinsman redeemer- a relative who, according to various laws of the Pentateuch, had the privilege or responsibility to act on behalf of a relative who was in trouble, danger, or need. The Hebrew term *'go el'* for 'kinsmen redeemer' designates one family member who delivers or rescues (Genesis 48:16, Exodus 6:6), or redeems property or person (Leviticus 27:9-25).

The movie plot brought to mind for me Deuteronomy 5:9-10, "...for I, the Lord your God, am a jealous God, visiting the iniquity of the fathers on the children, and on the third and the fourth generations of those who hate Me, but showing lovingkindness to thousands, to those who love Me and keep My commandments."

While the movie is about human trafficking, the only reason the girls find themselves in slavery to begin with is entirely due to their father's sin. This is a tangible example of iniquity and generational sin, whereby a future generation is led into slavery as a result of the sin(s) of former generations.

Jesus is now our kinsmen redeemer. When you give your life to Jesus Christ, it triggers a DNA paradigm shift in your lineage. Accepting Christ allows you to destroy darkness in your lineage, placed there by your ancestors. You can literally stand in the gap on their behalf and invoke the name of Jesus, through repentance, for your entire bloodline.

You can become a kinsmen redeemer for your family, birthing a kingdom alliance for future generations. Gideon was called to prepare an altar to the true living God in his own life before eventually destroying the altars of other gods that had been placed there by forefathers (Judges 6). We are called to do the same.

Let me put skin on this. After I rededicated my life to the Lord, I started attending a couple churches; mostly just trying desperately to feel clean, wishing I could hit the undo button on my life, and determined to never let anyone know the awful darkness in my past. I put on a brave smile as I attended a non-denominational church on Sundays, a highly charismatic cross-cultural church on Wednesdays, and charismatic revivals on Thursdays. I was desperate to put as much distance between myself and my past as possible. I was also severely thirsty for the truth.

A few months into my marathon church attendance, one of the churches I was going to had advertised an upcoming class titled, 'Freedom from Darkness'. If anyone needed freedom from darkness, it was me. The class covered everything from soul ties and open doors, witchcraft and the occult, to generational curses and iniquity. I had been shrouded in darkness for so long under the weight of my own sin and hurt, that the hunger for light and truth had become insatiable in me.

The class was structured with several weeks of content and teaching, laying the foundation for appropriating the power and grace of the cross on our life and our generational bloodline. At the end of those teaching weeks, each person had the opportunity to make an appointment with the pastors for an actual deliverance prayer session.

True to my nature, and my husband can attest to this, I couldn't wait several weeks to be free. Even though I had re-dedicated my life to the Lord, I still felt an incredible urgency to find freedom- still feeling shackled to everything behind me. I had been bound in darkness long enough. I tore through the content, gulping up every ounce of truth I had spent a lifetime being thirsty for.

When I made it to the section on generational iniquity, I wasn't sure what I needed to pray for, but I knew there were likely some things the Lord was wanting me to stand in the gap for. Desperate to be free but not really knowing the insight I needed, I asked the Lord to show me anything He wanted me to see and repent for. Though not sure exactly how He would do that, I was confident He was more than able to. True to His nature, He was faithful. The Lord revealed a couple things to me, through dreams and words of knowledge.

To be sure, as I wanted to know without a doubt that I was hearing from the Lord, I approached a family member about two different things the Lord had showed me regarding two family members who were no longer alive, hoping for confirmation of some sort. I will never forget the look on their face, turning sheet white as they asked me, "who told you? How could you possibly know about that?"

So, after running a couple dreams by family for confirmation, it became clear to me that the Lord was absolutely speaking through these dreams. I went to the store and bought a spiral notebook and started to document everything the Lord was showing me- continuing to ask Him for revelation until I had peace everything I needed to see, had been revealed.

As I said previously, I couldn't wait until the end of the class to be free. This had started to feel like a matter of life or death to me. So, I took my notebook filled with revelations the Lord had given me, and I headed to the park to pray. My notebook was so full of my sins and generational iniquity, that I sat at that park for hours praying.

I confessed the sins, broke agreements with the demonic spirits associated with those sins, pleaded the blood of Jesus on myself and my bloodline, and called forth the antithesis of those sins into my bloodline and blessings for future generations. Whew!

When I finished, I was exhausted. Hours of prayer and the fasting leading up to this day had left me spent. I decided to stop by the store on my way home from the park to grab some things I needed. To this day I can't remember what those items were. I reached the end of an aisle and was immediately arrested, visually.

I stood there completely frozen as I stared at a wall of towels. I began to sob. Yes, you read that right. I was crying over towels. Never in my life had I seen so many beautiful colors. It felt as though I was seeing color for the first time in my life and I was overwhelmed by it. I stood there, sputtering, "It's so beautiful. They're just so beautiful."

The confession session at the park had somehow transformed me. Though I couldn't put my finger on any tangible manifestation at the time, I was now a new person. I had just gone from scotoplo vision (night vision) to full spectrum vision. I was undone. I could not stop crying. The Lord had led me through the darkest valley and into His glorious light and for the first time in my life, I felt light.

As if that wasn't cool enough, I have more fun to share with you about this. I did not tell anyone in my class that I had jumped ahead, read through all the material, and prayed for deliverance on my own. Not because I thought I would be in trouble, it was simply important to me to be free, and this freedom was my own little treasure with the Lord.

I decided to still schedule my deliverance session with the pastors and prophetic ministers at the end of the class, even though I felt like I had already done business with the Lord. I reasoned more prayer is always a good thing and thought it was possible they could find or see something I had possibly overlooked.

Before my appointment, I was sent a piece of paper to fill out. Essentially it was a rap sheet. A comprehensive list of every sin you can imagine, with plenty of room for "fill in the blanks". To the side of the list, I checked different boxes, indicating whether that sin was specific to me, a family member, or both. I was brutally honest. Keep in mind, I still had not shared the park session with anyone.

As the day of my deliverance prayer session arrived, I walked into the room for my appointment, where the pastor and two prophetic ministers had already been in a prayer session regarding my appointment. Honestly, I wasn't sure what to expect as a lot of heavy sins and iniquity were on my rap sheet. I half expected to be chased out with stones thrown at me. Though I knew the Lord had forgiven me, I did not yet know if Christians could.

They asked me to sit down and then it started: "We can't make sense of this. We are reading over your summary and as you know, there's a lot of heavy stuff on here, but we don't feel any of it. It's as if it's a done deal already. As we prayed before you arrived, we just kept feeling the Lord's lightness and His thick presence of joy. His tangible presence is so thick in this room and when we prayed, we just saw this slippery surface, and nothing was able to grab hold of it because there was nothing left in your life for any darkness to cling to. We are trying to make sense of this."

What followed next was a long pause of wide-eyed blinking.

Praise God! Parks aren't just for kids.

So, what would have normally been a time of deliverance, became a time of releasing blessing. They covered me in prayer, released several prophetic words over my life, and sent me on my way, totally blessed.

"But you, when you pray, go into your room, and when you have shut your door, pray to your Father who is in the secret place; and your Father who sees in secret will reward you openly" (Matthew 6:6).

Now, why have I gone to such great lengths to share my testimony with you? I want you to understand that what you have done on your worst day is not your identity. It may be true that you are buried in darkness right now and can't find any tangible sign of light. But the truth is, you are fiercely loved by a King. A King who gave everything to ensure nothing could ever separate you from His Love, except by your own choice to do so. There is a difference between what is true about your current circumstances, and what is the truth about who you are.

I have also gone to great length to share my testimony with you because, if you'll remember, the word 'testimony' comes from a Hebrew word that means 'do again.' It is my earnest prayer that as people read this book, it will release creative power for the Lord to do it again. For me, 'beauty for ashes' is seeing someone else liberated because I was willing to humble myself, be vulnerable with a stranger, and share what the Lord has done for me.

Love is the greatest weapon, and it will be the power that destroys the works of darkness. It is the banner over His army.

"Come to me with your ears wide open. Listen, and you will find life. I will make an everlasting covenant with you. I will give you all the unfailing love I promised to David" (Isaiah 55:3; NLT).

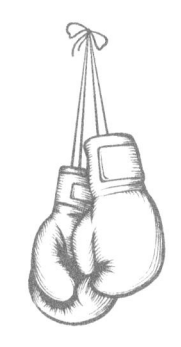

ADVANCING THE KINGDOM
Gaining Momentum

As we previously learned from Psalm 91, when we put our trust in Him, when we cling to Him, we are fully covered. When we do this, He becomes our refuge, as we are protected from the schemes of our enemies. We are safe from sickness and disease. We are victorious. We see His salvation.

We are going to look at this truth played out in 2 Chronicles 20. Jehoshaphat receives word that 'a great multitude' is coming to make war with him and Judah. "Jehoshaphat was afraid and turned his attention to seek the Lord and proclaimed a fast throughout all Judah. So, Judah gathered together to seek help from the Lord; they even came from all the cities of Judah to seek the Lord" (2 Chronicles 20:3-4).

Standing amidst all of Judah and Jerusalem, Jehoshaphat stands in the court and appeals to the Lord in heaven, "O Lord, the God of our fathers (reminding the Lord of their covenant), are You not God in the heavens? And are You not ruler over all the kingdoms of the nations? Power and might are in Your hand so that no one can stand against You. Did You not, O our God, drive out the inhabitants of this land before Your people Israel and give it to the descendants of Abraham Your friend forever?...See how they are rewarding us by coming to drive us out from Your possession which You have given us as an inheritance. O our God, will You not judge them? For we are powerless before this great multitude who are coming against us; nor do we know what to do, but our eyes are on You. All Judah was standing before the Lord, with their infants, their wives, and their children" (2 Chronicles 20:6-7,12-13).

Jehoshaphat is crying out to the Lord for help, and he's doing it by reminding the Lord of His covenant with them. He's calling on God's everlasting faithfulness, to yet again, be proven faithful. This is Jehoshaphat's only battleplan- and it's the only one he needs.

In response to this outcry, the Holy Spirit falls upon Jahaziel, a son of Zechariah. Jahaziel proclaims, "...'Do not fear or be dismayed because of this great multitude, for the battle is not yours but God's. Tomorrow go down against them. Behold, they will come up by the ascent of Ziz, and you will find them at the end of the valley in front of the wilderness of Jeruel. You need not fight in this battle; station yourselves, stand and see the salvation of the Lord on your behalf, O Judah and Jerusalem. Do not fear or be dismayed; tomorrow go out to face them, for the Lord is with you" (2 Chronicles 20:15-17).

This is an amazing passage of scripture. Not only do we see the power of the Holy Spirit manifested in the situation, but we also see the Lord declaring the battle is His and not theirs. Even though the battle is the Lord's, they must still go out and face the enemy. Then, He gives them the entire battle strategy and location of where the enemy will be. He totally exposes the enemy. It's no wonder the entire kingdom bowed in worship upon hearing this. In a few short sentences, God comforts, God directs, God exposes, God delivers, God saves.

The next morning, they rise early and head out to the wilderness. In verse 20 Jehoshaphat instructs them to, "put your trust in the Lord your God and you will be established. Put your trust in His prophets and succeed."

After this, Jehoshaphat sends the worshippers out ahead of the army. The Bible tells us that as soon as they began to praise the Lord (*yadah-* extend the hand), the Lord set ambushes against the enemy, and they were routed. In other words, as soon as they fixed their eyes on God and not the enemy, the Lord 'showed up.'

The Bible tells us the enemy destroyed itself. They all turned on each other and killed each other. When Judah approached the lookout of the wilderness to view the enemy, all they saw were corpses covering the ground. The Bible says not one escaped.

At this, they went down to gather the spoils of war. The Bible tells us there were so many treasures, it took them three days to gather the abundance. Then they returned to Jerusalem, overflowing with Joy for the Lord.

"They came to Jerusalem with harps, lyres and trumpets to the house of the Lord. And the dread of God was on all the kingdoms of the lands when they heard that the Lord had fought against the enemies of Israel. So, the kingdom of Jehoshaphat was at peace, for his God gave him rest on all sides" (2 Chronicles 20:28-29).

Remember, covenants are always for our benefit. Within them we find provision and our inheritance. The story of Jehoshaphat also teaches us that the Lord's covenants are eternal; that He will continue to fight for them as long as we partner with Him and fix our eyes on Him.

With this in mind, I believe it is now time to shift from a defensive posture of the body of Christ, to the offensive posture of the Bride of Christ. We have a mandate from the Lord to gather the exiles and to rebuild His family, to restore the former devastations. And we also have covenants with the Lord, ancient pathways, where we can fix our eyes on Him and appeal for His help.

I want to help illustrate what I mean by switching from a defensive posture to an offensive one. If I asked you who had more authority at a company, someone who had worked there for several years, or someone who had only worked there for two years, how would you answer?

You would likely respond by saying that while more information would be helpful, if forced to choose, you would select the person who had worked for the company longer. It's a logical choice.

If I asked you the same question but told you the person who had worked there for several years was the director of finance and the person who had only worked there for two years was an accounting clerk- which would you choose? You would logically select the director of finance as having more authority than the accounting clerk. It is an obvious choice.

If I told you the director of finance who had worked for the company for several years was an active new age wiccan and the accounting clerk who had only worked there for two years was a Christian, would it change your answer?

It should.

It just so happens the above scenario is part of my story. I was working for a company as an accounting clerk, while I was finishing up my senior internship for my undergraduate degree in counseling. My internship involved drafting a counseling program for a private Christian school, that currently had no counseling program.

To sustain both, I reported for work at the accounting job from 4am – 7am. Drove across town for my internship, from 7:30am-3pm. Then, returned to the other side of town and finished out my accounting job from 3:30pm-8:30pm.

My supervisor, the director of finance at the accounting job, was an active new age wiccan. She was incredibly smart at her job, with advanced degrees and had worked for the company for years. We managed to mostly work well together. However, as soon as I began interning at the Christian school, and my Christian faith appeared more evident, our working relationship became strained.

I found myself, on more than one occasion, being written up for supposed performance problems and errors. I was always able to provide clarity to the 'write ups,' explaining the decisions I had made and clearing the matter. Up until this point, I had only ever received glowing reviews and feedback on my job performance.

It was clear to me this was an all-out assault on me, as a believer in Christ. Literally a clash of kingdoms. The Bible is clear we do not war against flesh and blood but against principalities and forces of darkness in the spiritual realm (Ephesians 6:12).

Struggling with what to do about all of this, I processed the situation with a friend at the Christian school.

Her terse response was: "You know you have authority over that, right?"

That's it. That's all she said. No, "Oh, you poor thing, I'll be sure to pray for you tonight." Her brief pep-talk shot straight through me and I steadied my resolve. Sometimes we just need someone to remind us to put our combat boots on.

I arrived for work the following day, Thursday morning at 4am, as usual, armed with faith. I had a small vile of anointing oil and rubbed some on my finger. I prayed to anoint myself first, then I drew a line in the carpet with my finger, at the entrance of her office door, as well as the opening of my cubicle. Then I stood my ground and prayed that she would fall into the very trap she had set for me, and I asked the Lord for safe passage by. I declared authority over this attack in the name of Jesus and then prayed the Lord would open her eyes and asked Him to lead her to repentance and salvation.

That was it. Or at least that was all I knew to do. I went about the rest of my day as usual, driving across town to my internship, and then back to the office to wrap up my work for the night. I told no one about what I had done or prayed that morning, except for the friend who encouraged me to put my combat boots on.

The following Monday, as I returned to work from my internship, I was greeted with high-fives from different people in the company, all singing 'ding-dong, the wicked witch is gone!'

"WHAT?!" I asked, confused.

She was fired Friday evening, the day after I had prayed. No one in the company saw it coming, and she was especially blindsided. From what I was told, she didn't go without a fight either. The problem with that is the battle had already taken place in the spiritual realm the morning I prayed. It was a done deal. She had in fact, fallen into the very trap she had set for me and the Lord gave me safe passage by.

"For the godless nations get trapped in the very snares they set for others. The hidden trap they set for the weak has snapped shut upon themselves- guilty! The Lord is famous for this: his justice will punish the wicked. While they are digging a pit for others, they are actually setting the terms for their own judgment. They will fall into their own pit" (Psalm 9:15-16; TPT).

The word "overcomes" in this scripture is the Greek word *"nikao"* taken from the root word *"nike." Nikao* and *nike* are defined as 'to conquer, overcome, get the victory, conquest, a particular expression of victory, resulting from receiving (obeying) the faith Christ imparts.'

I like what J.H. Evans says, "Believers! Forget it not! You are the soldiers of the overcomer." As believers in Christ, it is our privilege to employ the victory of Jesus Christ on the earth. We are ambassadors of His light in this dark world.

"For whatever is born of God overcomes the world; and this is the victory that has overcome the world- our faith. Who is the one who overcomes the world, but he who believes that Jesus is the Son of God" (1 John 5:4-5)?

The example of my former wiccan boss is one of a defensive posture. Had she not decided to 'attack' me, I would have never risen to the fight. A modern-day example for me of David and

Goliath. We still need this in our artillery. However, I believe the Lord is now asking us to cross-over, or add to, our weaponry. We need the wholehearted mindset of Caleb. We need to change our posture from a defensive response of always deflecting punches thrown at us, to an offensive advance. I believe it is time to start taking territory back. To reclaim the former devastations. Let me share another powerful testimony with you to help illustrate this point.

There was a very large strip club right off the highway where I used to live. Before I had rededicated my life to Christ, I would feel disdain when I drove by it on my way to work, but ultimately helpless to really do anything about it. In fact, the thought that I even had an ability to do anything about it never crossed my mind.

After I rededicated my life to Christ, everything looked and felt different, including darkness. This strip club detested me even more now and I hated driving past it on the highway every day. I decided to start praying when I drove past it, asking God to burn the building to the ground. I prayed that it would happen in such a way that no one would be injured, and in such a way that it could not be rebuilt again.

I prayed this prayer twice a day as I drove past it, Monday through Friday. One day I happened to be daydreaming and was about to drive past it without praying. Suddenly, I heard the Holy Spirit boldly say, "LOOK!"

Startled, I shot my gaze toward the direction of the building. Where the building normally stood was a patch of burnt dirt. You should know that up to this point, I had been praying for seven years, hoping to see this happen. I immediately started crying and worshipping Jesus. I couldn't believe I had finally seen it happen!

I started asking everyone I could if they knew anything about what happened because I had specifically prayed that it would be burnt in such a way that it could not be rebuilt again and that no one would be hurt. Eventually, someone informed me they heard the owner had wanted to do an extensive remodel and decided it would be cheaper and faster to burn the building and rebuild what he wanted, than to try and remodel the whole structure.

I was so excited when I found this out because it meant not only was no one hurt, but it also meant the repairs would not be covered by insurance. So, I immediately started praying the owner's funds would dry up so it could not be rebuilt. To this day, the strip club has never been rebuilt. In fact, now in its place is a company that builds retaining walls.

Wikipedia explains retaining walls this way: "A retaining wall is a structure designed and constructed to resist the lateral pressure of soil, when there is a desired change in ground elevation that exceeds the angle of repose of the soil…The walls must resist the lateral pressures generated by loose soils."[35] In other words, retaining walls keep soil from eroding. Talk about a beautiful prophetic, redemptive picture of what the Lord did with this patch of dirt!

The above testimony is an offensive advance- taking territory for God's kingdom. We've been so focused on our programs, the lighting and fog machines, the logistics, etc.; we've lost sight of how to be the light, how to transform cities, nations, and atmospheres. The mandate was always to 'go;' we need to get back to a 'go' mindset.

Graham Cooke says, "One person walking with God is always in the majority." [36] He's right. It's time to reclaim territory for Jesus. It's time to offensively love people and the world around us. Matthew 11:12 tells us "…the Kingdom of Heaven has been forcefully advancing, and violent people are attacking it" (NLT).

"Lord, I will worship you with **extended hands** as my whole heart explodes with praise! I will tell everyone everywhere about your wonderful works and how your marvelous miracles exceed expectations! I will jump for you and shout in triumph as I sing your song and make music for the Most High God. For when you appear, **I worship while all of my enemies run in retreat**" (Psalm 9:1-2; TPT).

Whatever direction you are facing is the direction you will head in. The enemy knows that if he can keep you focused on your past, consumed by logistics, or buried in offenses, then he can keep you from stepping into your future. I know we need order, and these things serve a purpose- but in some ways, they've become our only purpose, and stripped us of our power and mission in the world.

Satan isn't afraid of your past, your programs, or your organizational skills. But he is terrified of your future. Remember, the Lord isn't focused on the enemy or our sin. God knows that what you need more than anything is to focus on His love. His love is a powerhouse for your life. It is a catalyst for internal transformation- the fruit of which is external radiance in the world around you. Remember, battles are never about circumstances. Battles are about trust, and trust is built on covenant.

"You have wrapped me in power, and now you've shared with me your perfection. Through you I ascend to the highest peaks of your glory to stand in the heavenly places, strong and secure in you. You've trained me with the weapons of warfare-worship; now I'll descend into battle with power to chase and conquer my foes. You empower me for victory with your wrap-around presence. Your power within makes me strong to subdue, and by stooping down in gentleness you strengthened me and made me great! You've set me free from captivity and now I'm standing complete, ready to fight some more" (Psalm 18:32-36; TPT)!

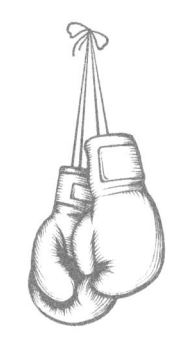

PACKING A PUNCH, AN EPILOGUE-
A Journey In Prayer

I do not believe there is only one way to pray something. Prayer is not about a formula. The Lord is deeply aware of our motivations and intentions, which fuel our prayers. With that said, sometimes we need a little help. Sometimes we just need something tangible to help us find our own words. This chapter is about that.

It is important that you speak these prayers out loud. As we have discussed in this book, there is too much power in the spoken word (ruach) and testimony of Jesus, to pass up an opportunity to decree these things into the atmosphere.

I hope this chapter helps you to find your own voice. I hope it helps to ignite the deep embers in your heart- embers that burn to encounter the heartbeat of God. I hope it unleashes the sword of your testimony, wrecking violence on the giants squatting in your land- your inheritance.

"And I will give you the keys of the Kingdom of Heaven, and whatever you bind on earth will be bound in Heaven, and whatever you loose on earth is loosed in Heaven" (Matthew 16:19)

Prayer Of Salvation

If you have not accepted Jesus Christ into your heart yet or would like to renew that commitment, this is the best place to start. This prayer of faith is the gateway to eternal life and to living a life of victory and fullness in the earth.

Romans 10:9-10 says that if we confess with our mouths that Jesus is Lord and believe in our hearts that God raised Him from the dead, we will be saved. With our hearts, we believe and are justified. With our mouths, we confess and are saved.

"Dear Lord Jesus, I know that I am a sinner, and I ask for Your forgiveness. I believe You died for my sins and rose from the dead. I turn from my sins and invite You to come into my heart and life. I want to trust and follow You as my Lord and Savior."

Prayer For Baptism Of The Holy Spirit

The baptism of the Holy Spirit is for every believer. We receive it in the same way that we received salvation – through faith. Jesus promised us the Holy Spirit, and in fact said it was for our benefit for Jesus to ascend to Heaven so He could send us the Holy Spirit, our helper.

Not asking for the baptism of the Holy Spirit, is like entering a gun fight with a knife. You aren't going to last long, and if you do, it won't be without the need for serious triage. The Holy Spirit empowers us to accomplish everything the Father has intended for our lives. Don't miss this precious opportunity to accept such a power, precious, and free gift.

"Father, I come to You in Jesus name, desiring the baptism of Your Holy Spirit. Your word says that I can have it, and I believe what You have said. I receive this gift by faith in Jesus' name. I thank You Father for this precious and power gift."

PRAYER- KNITTING OF SOULS

Soul ties, healthy and destructive, are emotional bonds that become attachments in our lives. We were created for relationships, with God and humans. Godly soul ties are the bonds that enrich our lives. Ungodly soul ties, to a person, place, or thing, have the power to enslave us to less than God's best for our lives. The influence of ungodly soul ties can lead to oppression, bad decisions, and despair. 2 Peter 2:19 tells us that we are slaves to anything that controls us.

An easy place to do inventory on this is past romantic relationships and/or destructive friendships or partnerships. Ask the Holy Spirit for revelation on any other person, place, or thing that may also need to be included.

"Father, if my soul has been knit or bound to the soul of any of the following people, places, or things, in any manner that is not of You and would not bring glory and honor to the Lord Jesus Christ, I ask You to forgive me. Forgive me if I have put that person, place, or thing, before You, and looked to it to meet my needs rather than You. I confess that as sin and repent of the sin of idolatry. According to Your word in Matthew 16:19, You have given me authority to loose my soul from all ungodly or unhealthy ties in which the enemy has bound my soul.

I choose to loose my soul from the soul of each of the following:

_____

_____

_____

_____

Forgive me if I have held any unforgiveness toward any of these people. As best I know, I choose to forgive them for any way

they may have sinned against me. I ask You also to forgive me for any way in which I have sinned against them. I bless them and I ask You to bless them with Your truth that will set them free.

If, according to Your wisdom and knowledge, I have not genuinely forgiven any of them, I'm asking You to reveal that to me and to prepare me and enable me to truly forgive each one of them. I choose to allow You to produce in me that attitude toward the that the Lord Jesus Christ wants me to have.

If I have listened to any lies that Satan or any demonic forces have given me concerning any of these people, I confess that as sin, and I ask You to forgive me. I now break agreements with those lies. I loose myself from all claims, ties, holds, and judgements these people may have had against me.

Father, I ask You to destroy and render powerless every demon that has been afflicting me because of these lies. I ask You to cleanse me with Your Blood from all effects and any defilement these ungodly ties and alignments produced. I ask that You would restore to me Godly and healthy relationships. I put the blood of Jesus Christ between me and each person I have named and any demons that may be in or around them.

All this I pray in the name, power, and authority of the Lord Jesus Christ."[37]

References: 1 Samuel 18:1, Colossians 2:2, Job 22:28, Isaiah 54:17

Prayer Of Surrender

A prayer of surrender is a great place to start when you need to renew your commitment to the Lord, or when you want to deepen that commitment. Surrendering our life to the Lord and inviting Him into our hearts to heal and restore is a precious gift.

"Father, I come to You in Jesus' name. I confess all of my known sins to you, God. I repent of these sins and turn away from them. Please wash me and cleanse me with the blood of Jesus. Now I confess all my unknown sins to you, God. I repent of these sins also. I turn away from them. Please wash me and cleanse me with the blood of Jesus.

Now I expose every lie and agreement with the enemy in my life. I break these agreements, and these lies in the authority of Jesus' name. I forbid any of Satan's works and presence to continue in my life. I resist them all now in the authority of Jesus' name. I am the temple of the Holy Spirit, bought by the blood of Jesus. Thank you, Lord Jesus, for cleansing me with Your precious blood.

Now Lord Jesus, please seal my mind with Your precious blood. Please seal my emotions and my will with Your precious blood. Please seal my body, soul, and spirit with Your precious blood. Please seal my heart, and my very person, with Your precious blood. Thank you, Lord Jesus, for sealing every part of my life with your precious blood. I choose to release all of my control to You Lord Jesus, and no one else is allowed to control me. You are my Lord, Jesus. The battle belongs to You, Lord Jesus. I give you control of my life. I submit myself to You, Lord Jesus."[38]

PRAYER AGAINST TRAFFICKING – FRIENDLY FIRE

As a result of living in a fallen world, and the vulnerabilities of our humanity, we may occasionally find ourselves under unintended oppression from someone else. Another term for this is 'friendly fire.' The Bible says our words carry life and death and there is great power in the tongue. (Proverbs 18:21) Because of this, when we slander, gossip, or carry offenses against people, we project that negativity into the atmosphere. That negativity becomes a dagger in the hand of the enemy to torment and oppress our ourselves and our fellow humans.

"Lord Jesus, please have your warring angels come and remove from me all people who are trafficking on me- those born of Your spirit as well as those who are not.

If I have given place for people to traffick on me through unhealthy or ungodly soul ties or agreements that are not from You, I ask You to forgive me. I choose to loose my soul from them and break any ungodly agreements I have made with them. I sever all claims, ties and holds they may have over me. Please bring them before Your throne and show them that You are the only one allowed headship over me.

According to Isaiah 54:17, I condemn every judgment that may have been spoken against me by these people. I declare that You alone, Lord Jesus, are my Lord and no one else is allowed to lord over me. Please have Your warring angels seal each person that has been trafficking on me back to their own body. I put the blood of Jesus between all these people and me and forbid them to return to me in the authority of Jesus' mighty name."[39]

References: Matthew 16:19, Job 22:28, Isaiah 54:17, Psalms 5:12, 2 Corinthians 10:13

PRAYER AGAINST TRAFFICKING – THE OCCULT AND WITCHCRAFT

We face an enemy that hates us with a malevolence that is unparalleled. Satan and his cohorts have unfortunately deceived a multitude, and his boldness of attack is more prevalent than ever before. The Bible is clear that we do not battle against flesh and blood (humans) but against spiritual forces of evil. (Ephesians 6:12)

While our battle is not against flesh and blood, Satan uses the occult to wreck oppression, on those bound to darkness and on believers alike. This is not something we need to fear. We have authority over this in the name and blood of Jesus.

"In the authority of the name of the Lord Jesus Christ and by the power of His Blood, I cancel all astral assignments over my life. I take dominion over all demons that have given assignments to those in the occult or those involved in witchcraft to traffick on me or afflict me in any way. I render powerless and destroy these demons and their assignments by the power of the Blood of the Lord Jesus Christ.

Lord, according to Your word in Isaiah 54:17, I condemn, cancel out and destroy all judgments, assignments, curses, and rituals that may have been spoken or done against me, and decree no weapon formed against me shall prosper.

Lord, please have your warring angels seal each person who has been trafficking on me back to their own body. I put the blood of Jesus between these people and me and forbid them to return to me in the authority of Jesus' mighty name. I ask you, Lord, to reveal to them the deception of Satan over their lives and the truth of Your great love for them and Your plan to set them free. I ask that each one come into the saving knowledge of the Lord Jesus Christ and receive You as their Lord and Savior. Lord, please establish your shields of protection over me."[40]

References: Matthew 16:19, Job 22:28, Isaiah 54:17, Psalms 5:12, 2 Corinthians 10:13

PRAYER OF THANKSGIVING

It is good to remember all that the Lord has done for us. Offering praise to Him for His love and faithfulness is a sweet aroma to the Lord. It is also important to acknowledge and thank the Lord for His protection and His provision in our lives. The following prayer seeks to accomplish both.

"I stand in the name of the Lord Jesus Christ of Nazareth who came in the flesh and I thank You for binding all retaliations, reactions, and revenge of Satan for me, my family, our property, and anything to do with our lives. I thank You for binding all future assignments, all equipment, traps, tripwires, curses, equipment, channels, backups, and replacements with Your blood, Lord Jesus. I ask that you nullify and destroy any rotten fruit this has produced in my life or anyone around me. Thank you for sealing them all up, rendering them powerless, destroying them, and sending them into the abyss.

Father God, I thank You for releasing Your blessings, love, healing, deliverance, and truth into my life. Thank You for renewing my mind with Your wisdom. Thank You for Your anointing and provision in every area of my life. Thank You for having Your mighty warring angels stand guard all around me and for preparing the way before me. Thank You, Lord Jesus, for this mighty work of deliverance and healing in my life. Thank You for releasing me into all the gifts and the calling You have given me." [41]

POWERHOUSE PRAYER

I saved the best for last. This last prayer is so incredible and powerful- you can say it in any circumstance, as loud as you want, and as often as you want. It will yield more than you could ever imagine.

"JESUS!"

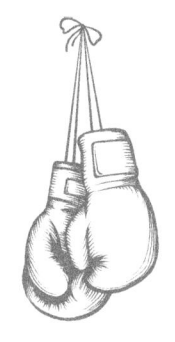

Endnotes

1. Mike Bickle. 2014. Studies in the Song of Solomon. Page 13.
2. John Piper. 1983. God's Covenant with David.
3. Aftermath Services. 2017. The Stages of Human Decomposition.
4. Dutch Sheets Sermon. 2019. Judah, Extending of the Hands.
5. Rick Clendenen. 2006. Mentoring from the Mountaintop.
6. Dutch Sheets Sermon. 2019. Judah, Extending of the Hands.
7. Bible Hub. 2004-2020. Hebrew 1661.
8. Alex Russan. 2019. The Science of Tannins in Wine.
9. Bible Study Tool. 1897. Dictionary-anakim.
10. J. Hampton Keathley III. 2004. The Captain of the Lord's Army.
11. J. Hampton Keathley III. 2004. The Captain of the Lord's Army.
12. Dutch Sheets Sermon. Air Supremacy.
13. Bible Study Tools. 1992-2020. Greek/Hebrew Definitions.
14. Kyle Mantyla. 2017. A Prophetic Sign About Ending Abortion

15 Marilette Sanches. 2017. 'Wonder Woman' Might Be the Most Accurate On-Screen Depiction of Biblical Womanhood, And Here's Why

16 Julie Herrer-Maxwell. 2016. Deborah.

17 Mike Bickle. 2014. Studies in the Song of Solomon. Page 7.

18 Mike Bickle. 2014. Studies in the Song of Solomon. Page 22.

19 Bible Hub. 2004-2020. Hebrew/5401.

20 Brene Brown. 2014. Listening to Shame.

21 Kris Vallotton. 2019. 5 Concerning Cultural Side Effects of our Fatherless Generation.

22 Casey Chalk. 2019. Va. Public School Indoctrinates 5-Year-Olds About Transgenderism Without Telling Parents.

23 Helen. Raleigh. 2019. Over Parent Objections, Public School Teaches 6-Year-Olds About 'Transgender Ravens' And Gender Fluidity.

24 Gregory Korte. 2016. Schools must allow transgender bathrooms, Department of Education says.

25 National File. 2020. Report: California 8th Graders Taught Anal, Bondage, Sex Involving Blood in Sex-Ed Class.

26 Cal Thomas. 2016. Transgender bathroom 'guidance' could be last straw: Cal Thomas.

27 Dr. Judith Reisman. 2010. Table 34.

28 Judith Reisman. 2017. Rockefeller's Legacy: Enabling Sexual Revolution.

29 Steve Warren. 2020. America's First Non-Binary Person Admits 'Big Mistake,' Legally Changes Back to Male.

30 Mike Bickle. 2014. Studies in the Song of Solomon. Page 29-30.

31 The Passion Translation. 2017. Song of Songs 4.

32 The Century Dictionary. 1891. Twining.

33 Merriam-Webster.com Dictionary, s.v. "domino effect," accessed February 24, 2020, https://www.merriam-webster.com/dictionary/domino%20effect.

34 The Passion Translation. 2017. Acts 4:31.

35 Wikipedia. 2020. Retaining Wall.

36 Graham Cooke. 2016. The Practice of Delight.

37 Faith Bible Chapel. 2006 Freedom from Darkness.

38 Faith Bible Chapel. 2006. Freedom from Darkness.

39 Faith Bible Chapel. 2006. Freedom from Darkness.

40 Faith Bible Chapel. 2006. Freedom from Darkness.

41 Faith Bible Chapel. 2006. Freedom from Darkness.

CPSIA information can be obtained
at www.ICGtesting.com
Printed in the USA
LVHW081547180320
650460LV00009B/836

9 781630 509606